WILL
IT
WOW?

EMBRACE | FOCUS | DISRUPT

WILL IT WOW?

HOW TO DESIGN PRODUCTS PEOPLE LOVE

CHUNSHIK KIM

ISBN 9798663538657

Printed in the United States of America
Cover design by Chunshik Kim

First Edition

PROLOGUE

Being a consumer was pretty amazing. We've got to choose products desperately or impulsively. Seeing countless product choices in the mall, my passion for 'product design' was formed in South Korea where I was born, and led me to a job interview with one the greatest product design agency, Ziba, located in Portland, Oregon. After two years of tedious interview process, the offer made our family move to the US to explore the one of the largest consumers and the corporate brands in North America. I was with two-year-old boy and my wife being 8-months pregnant. It sounds still crazy!

Settling down in the US took a while as we found an apartment and filled the space with new stuffs. From consumer electronics to a car, the buying experience was fund, but took time to justify our decision. Being parents of two was completely changing our behavior and decision on the shopping list. It was our golden-time as consumers and down-to-earth parents. Meanwhile, I was exploring new product developments every day at the studio. I have designed multiple products and developed handful corporate design languages that impacts our clients' business success.

As my career evolved, the way I viewed products both at home and at work grew to the point where I needed to change. As we moved to Silicon Valley, California, my growing children made our house feel much smaller, and this made us change the game plan. I happened to look at what is essential to everyday life and what truly brings us value and joy. This question became the birthplace of 'WILL IT WOW?'. And, I found this can a great chance to measure the value of the products we are facing every day.

I hope that 'WILL IT WOW?' can find a common ground with your perspective, and together we will be able to design beautiful and meaningful products that make our planet the better place to live.

Designer
Chunshik Kim

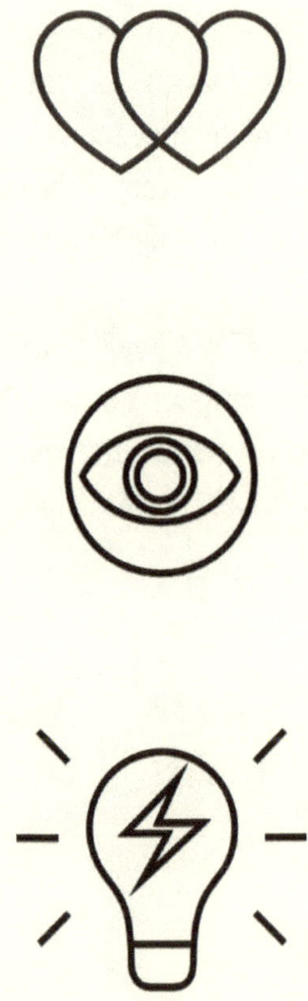

CONTENTS

Part 1: EMBRACE

Part 2: FOCUS

Part 3: DISRUPT

WILL IT WOW?

HOW TO DESIGN PRODUCTS PEOPLE LOVE

INTRODUCTION

Every year, 30,000 new products are introduced to the market. [1] Surprisingly, "about half of all resources invested in product development and commercialization in the U.S. goes to products that are canceled or fail to yield an adequate financial return,"[2] said R G. Cooper, an established economic expert. He estimated the product failure at 48% in his book, 'Winning at New Products,' as other researchers typically count higher. So why are they crashing, and what causes a lack of success? This is most likely the consequence for three reasons: failure to understand the consumer, poor product quality, and lack of internal capability. [3] Witnessing the countless developers failing to bring their products to market, leads me to ask three questions:

1. Who are the consumers today and how do we characterize their reason for a better life?
2. How do great companies develop their product for success?

---

[1] Harvard Business School professor Clayton Christensen
[2] Robert G Cooper, "Winning at New Products"
[3] Neil Patel, "90% of Startups fail."

3. What does a fast-growing company do to be a firm starter and stay healthy in the market?

It is imperative that product developers ask these three questions for the greatest chance of product survival in markets inundated with competitor products.

Companies are trying to make a meaningful bond with consumers and a strong connection to users. In order to meet users in the growing market and win their loyalty, product developers must learn about the consumers' needs. Accurately understanding these needs is what motivates great products. Product Development Teams must be nimble to adopt changes in the market.

While companies are still baby-stepping into the new market, agile disruptors are already engaging, focusing, and pioneering the consumer market. By mastering the simple three steps, you can design a great product that is indispensable.

Unlike goods produced during the mass production era of the 1920s, today's successors are embracing their consumers' actual needs. They look inside the consumers' minds to pull out the desire instead of fixing non-existent problems. They bring the simplest product solutions that focus on the essentials instead of distracting consumers with complex features. Startups utilize the overlaps of *role* and *responsibility* to achieve a passionate business goal rather than working only what is expected.

How I Got Onboard

My eyes were opened to the business of industrial design when I joined the MID (Master of Industrial Design) program at Pratt Institute. I learned that humans pursue what is emotionally touching regardless of times, cultures and ages. We desire meaningful objects for a better life. Emotion is the most powerful way to make a meaningful connection with consumers.

I was lucky to start my first career as a hands-on designer at Samsung Corporate Design Center located in Korea. This is where I learned and practiced production-ready design, which is how to minimize the gap between a design concept and production. Knowing what is doable and what is challenging had provided me insights on how to prioritize projects. Ziba[4] was my birthplace for connecting with consumers. Sitting with consumers on-site at their home or in research facilities allowed me to hear directly what they love and hate in a

---

[4] Design consulting agency, based in Portland, OR, USA

product. This opportunity to listen to the actual needs of consumers and debrief their thoughts was a game-changer. In addition, working at the core of Silicon Valley matured my career to leverage the collaboration, efficiency, and speed that all contributes to successful product development.

While I look back at how the creative processes evolved in my career, I concluded 'the EFD model' (Embrace, Focus, and Disrupt), to develop a quality product that makes our consumers' lives better. With the EFD model, a product can be well engineered and thoughtfully designed to enhance the user's life, and bring an adequate return for the developers and the brand.

EFD Model

After 20 years of product development experience, I realized that there is always a right design process to enhance a quality product. The EFD model will help you to work purposefully and save time in process. This process will also help to maximize the resource you already have to reach the business goal.

PART 1: Embrace

Embrace is a compassionate approach to understand who are the consumers today. They are the reason for bringing products and services into the world. Identifying consumers' pain-points reveals opportunities in the market. It is crucial to understand the role of authenticity and community connection among Millennials, as these new consumers will directly disrupt the consumer market.

PART 2: Focus

The market is inundated with products. We can buy anything we can possibly imagine. The problem is that only a small portion of these products provide us with a quality experience. Great companies hire talented team members to create the design rationale. Braun [5] , had established strong design principles by the development team. The principles not only changed the entire product line for Braun, but later it influenced other companies like Apple. Quality design matters, especially since it makes a significant impact when it works consistently in the production line.

---

[5] German consumer products company based in Kornberg. From 1984 until 2007

PART 3: Disrupt

> The 2020 CES (Consumer Electronics Show) hosted more than 1,200 startups to 'Eureka Park,' a birthplace of future technologies. CES can be viewed as a blueprint, unveiling where the market trends go, and how they disrupt technology and its execution. Startups are fast and agile to react to the market changes. It is great to see what fast-growing companies do to survive and how they adopt changes to stay healthy in the market.

In this book, I will address the logic behind design development using the EFD model. Part 1 will talk about consumers and their journeys. Part 2 will share a comprehensive way to focus on problems that the corporate design team and the design agencies are using for quality products. In Part 3, you will learn how to find clues about new technologies in product development in Silicon Valley and how to disrupt the development process to yield a successful product. My small goal here is to share the design ingredients so that you can develop your own 'Design Recipe' for your product to succeed.

Illustration by Ellie Kim, 10th Grader

WHAT IS DESIGN RECIPE?

Design Recipe

In our society, design indicates comprehensive action that relates to creating something new and purposeful. Whether the activity is about developing a product or service, the job requires a creative approach to fulfill the purpose. Functional design works when a product delivers a physical benefit for users, while emotional design only works when it reflects an individual desire.

The aesthetic is an intrinsic part of the design. Nonetheless, not all design activities consider beauty as a core element, while others emphasize the artistic value in many different ways. Beauty has its energy, influencing our lives. The beautifully designed Nespresso machine, for example, proudly becomes an art piece in the kitchen. The pod storage next to the machine perfectly organizes various flavors for the users to choose for the day. Thus, aesthetic products not only make consumers happy, but it makes a daily ritual more enjoyable.

The impact is hard to measure but extremely valuable. Aesthetics in design is a significant element that reflects a connection between products and consumers. The value of the relationship may be abstract and challenging to visualize. That is one of the reasons why the aesthetic value is often not taken into as much consideration as it should deserve.

Design Recipe is about design with intrinsic values that matter for our daily lives. It is exciting to witness how industrial technology has evolved into digital and how software dominates over hardware. The software industry is making significant growth in product development while other enterprises try to catch up. However, the aesthetic value of hardware and software excels when they synchronize together. The joint efforts require building a bridge where hardware and software designers work together to elevate the design's value.

This book will refer to 'the practical design principles' that have been successfully implemented in the field and encourage more developers to use those experiences in various design activities. For product designers, Design Recipe will show how design can initiate great thinking for its purpose.

Creative thinkers arise from great motivation and a disruptive mindset. This book will provide comprehensive activities that not only connect the people but also help businesses grow. Successful design always has a great story to tell, and Design Recipe will help to kick off your own design story.

Anyone Can Design

Anyone can be a designer. Any purposeful intention to make our lives better can be a healthy design seed to yield a successful and profitable product. In a professional setting, however, the design should be a collaborative effort in the search for common interests and purposes. Design Recipe will cover a significant number of aspects that can facilitate design development. It will be useful for a variety of individuals, from students to professionals, or from startups to large corporations as it delivers core design principles that can universally improve design quality.

As I have gone through design school, corporate roles, and consultancy in my career, I have realized that many design teams are struggling with lack of direction, or understanding of how to visualize the consumer's needs. Each organization has its strength and weaknesses. For example, a team connects to the target consumers really well to understand the needs, but has poor concept visualization, whereas the other team has a strong design team but does not understand their consumers. As a result, we witness great products failing because they try to solve non-existent problems. Design Recipe will highlight design tools and aspects to fill the gap and strengthen what you already have. As a guidebook, Design Recipe will use industry terminology that everyone can share and leverage for their use.

How to Use This Book

As professional design requires collaborative efforts for a common goal, it requires a design process. The process usually consists of resources, milestones, and schedules. The timeline, as they typically call it 'the phase,' identifies individual goals to achieve. Each phase needs its tools and focal points. Each phase also requires different team members and approaches. For example, the design exploration phase should relate more to consumer experiences, whereas the refinement phase requires significant work on the production aspects.

As you already found on the cover of this book, I break the design recipe into three parts: Embrace, Focus, and Disrupt. These three parts represent the three different mindsets product developers can use to maximize the goal of each phase. Each section follows with a handful of tools and insights the team can utilize depending on needs. For example, the marketing team can focus on Part1: EMBRACE in search of their strategic consumers. In contrast, the engineering team can find Part3: DISRUPT useful to encourage a creative and innovative approach. For designers, as they are middlemen to bridge between business and technology, so all parts are critical. I would encourage you to frame the three steps as a spine of your design process and select the bullet points on each step as you plan your project. Each stage will allow your team to frame a unique and productive design process to result in successful output.

There is no right or wrong process. The right process is that one that is flexible enough to fit the needs of the product development team. The successful design is not the one the most beautiful one to survive, nor the most intellectual, but the most responsive to adapt to the consumers.

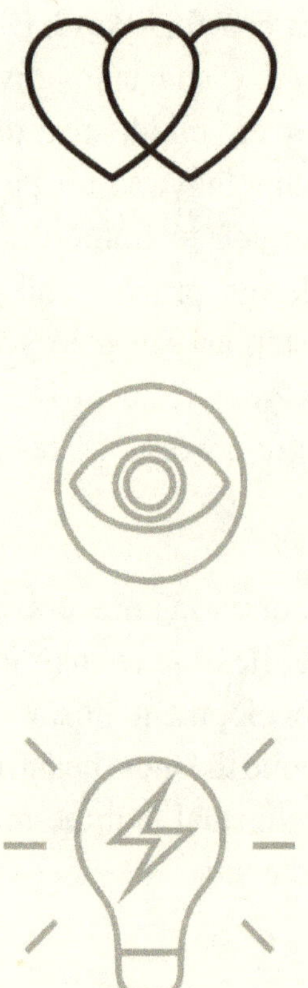

| PART 1 |

EMBRACE EMOTION

*"You can't understand good design
if you don't understand people."*[6]
-Dieter Rams

---

[6] Less and More: The Design Ethos of Dieter Rams by Dieter
Rams

Part 1: EMBRACE

01_ CONSUMER

02_ DESIRE

03_ EGO TO ECO

04_ EMPATHY

01 _CONSUMER

Unlike users, consumers refer to people who look for products and services for their needs and desires. What makes them peculiar in comparison to users is that they have the power to possess the commodity. They are one of the primary motivators for all design activities. They are the reason for most of the business, and for whom product developers work hard to make their world a better place.

Consumers are king. They are so powerful that they can change the way businesses run. Each generation has a unique value proposition and should be reached and understood uniquely. Therefore, understanding who they are will provide designers fundamental ideas to develop essential products, and as a result, the product will be able to survive in the market. In addition to that, the survivor can open up a new business opportunity for which designers can repeatedly compete for better service. Designers are encouraged to understand consumer experiences as a pattern. Typically, they call the pattern the Consumer Journey.

Journey

Consumer Journey refers to what consumers experience throughout the entire product and service experience. To help designers understand the experience better, they often create a map that visualizes the experience as a repeating pattern. The Customer Journey Map (Figure 1) typically illustrates the complete consumer experience. It begins with the purchasing experience and ends with disposal. The process breaks the whole journey into individual steps. Looking closely at each phase can reveal new design opportunities and is often instrumental in developing new products that may not happen otherwise.

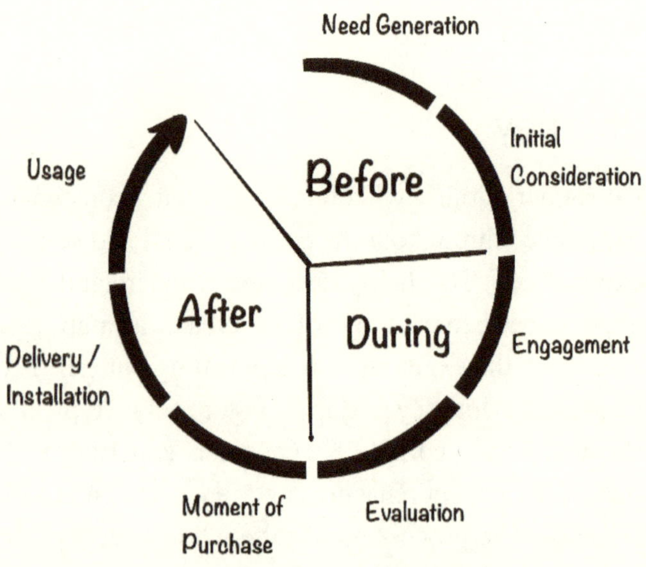

Figure1 Consumer Journey Map

Persona

In a retail store, products overwhelm consumers. Furthermore, there are hundreds of products on the shelves screaming for people's attention. For example, beauty products such as cosmetics are strategically appealing to the specific target consumers while differentiating from the competitors. Understanding consumers' characteristics is often complicated. In an ideal retail store, consumers are unknowingly looking at clustered products that characterize them.

Sephora, a multinational chain of personal care and beauty stores, targets consumers on the mainstream beauty market with approachable characteristics of its brand, like eye-catching products that appeal to pre-teens to young adults with approachable and friendly design elements. In contrast, Glossier, a skincare and beauty product store, focuses on the natural and revolutionary characters in a similar category. These are companies that use two distinctive personal characteristics on products to appeal to their strategic consumer group. These characteristics can reflect the target consumers' persona and lifestyle. For another example, Procter & Gamble[7] personifies their customer groups based on their attributes that identify the product images. The product images strategically manipulate into multiple clusters, and each group uses its representative visual characteristics to appeal to the targeted groups. These product images characterize specific consumers, and the personalized image repeats in the same product line as a design language. For example, geometric visual elements are used to appeal to consumers who care about function features and its' performance, while vibrant and

---

[7] American multinational consumer goods corporation founded in 1837

aesthetic images are utilized to approach to the group who cares about beauty and fashion.

Can Design Personify?

The answer will be clear when designers meet consumers and listen to what they say. To achieve a successful consumer product, designers need to observe consumer's lifestyles to identify their personalities. 'Consumer research' can take this part. Even if there is little time or resource available for research, designers are still encouraged to do quick secondary research through web searches or books and magazines that are related to target consumers. Through research, designers can start to personify a target consumers' lifestyle. Designers can bring the personified images and attributes into the ideation session which can translate to crucial design elements. It is always helpful if the consumer attributes, as research debrief, can transform into visual images or 3-dimensional forms. The output will help the design team to verify how the personified design elements can integrate with the product.

Research

Design development can yield better ideas with research on the target consumers than starting ones straight from a sketch board. There are two types of consumer research. One is visiting the consumers' home, and the other is a focus group where a group of interviewees participates in a facility. Visiting homes is a great way to legitimately see the target consumer's lifestyle and personality in depth. At the same time, a focus group is practical to create design ideas from multiple conversations. The former is an excellent way for designers to personify consumers' characteristics. The latter will be useful to capture their reaction by sharing various design concepts.

Ethnographic design research is concerned with understanding individuals in the context of their daily lives and framing their behaviors within the environment and community that surrounds them.[8] Through the research, the design team can take a survey on consumer insights collected to prioritize strong concepts.

---

[8] A Designer's Research Manual

The most critical part of the research is revealing what the team does not know. The team should find the knowledge gap and be able to fill the unknown elements with primary learning from the research. Recruiting the right people is always a challenge, but crucial to the success of the research activity. It is always helpful to select more people and filter them through a quick conversation to select final interviewees.

Experience

Consumer's sequential experience with products takes three steps. The adventure begins with Attract that triggers human sense to pay attention to objects on shelves. The attraction must be simple yet strong enough to do the job. Once attracted, the product starts to Engage with users. The users' experience and interaction now play their roles, and the engagement repeatedly happens throughout the product's lifetime. The last step is to Extend. It is about leaving an impression on the users beyond the product's functional benefit. This impression will be instrumental if it is strong enough for the user to remember and make a personal connection to it. Designers should be able to extend the product experience. This is a continuing opportunity to retain the existing consumers with a consistent product and brand experience.

During product development, the team creates design elements that speak to consumers. Some details are visually screaming, while others show calmly. When consumers face these products, they perceive the design parts to react. During the creative process, those reactions can be referred and manipulated by taking a close look at individual behaviors in sequence. The exercise can officially run by consumer research, which is always a productive investment.

Design elements also communicate through the course of a consumer journey from purchase to disposal. The parts have intrinsic energy to draw the very first attention to the customers in the retail environments, and the consumer journey physically starts from there. Again, the journey takes three steps: Attract, Engage, and Extend. (Figure 2) But how can designers ensure that the three steps are useful?

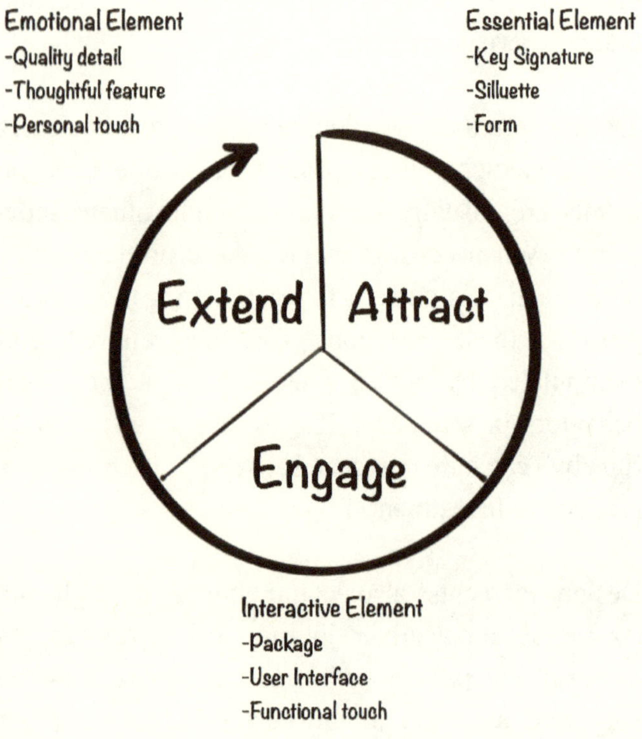

Figure2 Consumer Experience 360

Attract

The product consists of multiple design elements, and not all of them attract consumers at once in the retail environment. Amongst many competitors' products, it is crucial to demonstrate what primary design element initially draws attention from consumers. The big idea features a part that highlights primary functional benefits, such as a central user interface and an iconic form. "Attract" is the beginning of the design journey, setting up the first impression of the product. "There is nothing to promise without the attraction, just like nothing to cook without the fishing."

Engage

Once attraction is complete, then customers become users. Some products emphasize this phase on the packaging to elevate the product experiences, which are essential to reassure consumers' buying decisions. The user engagement begins from the unboxing experience. This is the point when users touch the product and start to interact with what it offers. All the functional benefits and practicality of the product service take place in the engagement phase. This practical user experience is, for sure, a critical point in which consumers judge whether or not the product is functioning the way they expected.

Consumers in today's market are smart and critical, and do not hesitate to share their opinions with their community. This is the timeframe when unqualified products and services will not stay in the market for that reason. In other words, a product that exceeds the users' expectation will successfully engage with its users and others.

During this "Engage" process, users likely make up their minds on whether they love or hate the product. It is a significant moment in the relationship between the product and user, which in the case of an excellent product experience can yield the inception of 'brand royalty'.

Extend

The last step is about how to extend the relationship between the product and the user. This step focuses on how to make consumers continue engaging with the product and brand positively so that they come back and bring more consumers with them. So how does Extend work? There are many ways to retain the product and user relationship. Users are often impressed by thoughtful touches discovered throughout the product experience. It is all about the design element that creates an 'emotional connection' to the consumers.

The OXO[9] angled measuring cup (Figure 3) is a great example of thoughtful design features that inspire engaged followers. The tool features a brilliant idea of indicating measures inside the bowl in a user-friendly viewing angle. Users can read numbers straight from the top without bending over to see them from the side. The idea that pulls out the traditional inconvenience, which most users probably would not think about. The $9 kitchen tool not only helps users read the measurements painlessly but makes the cooking experience more enjoyable. Furthermore, the innovative design idea makes users perceive the brand as creative and memorable.

---

[9] American manufacturer of kitchen utensils and problem-solving tools that make every day better.

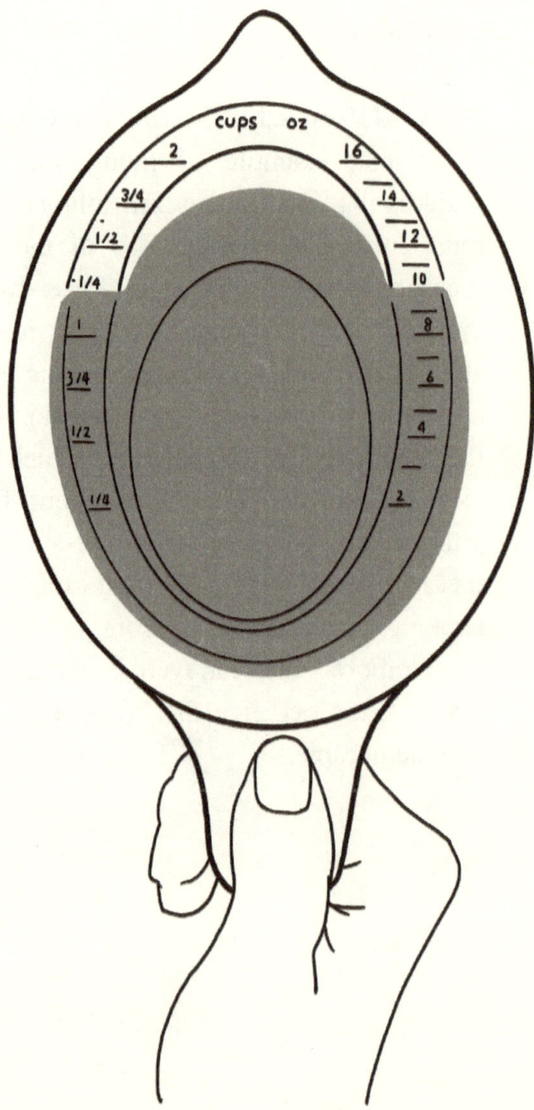

Figure 3 OXO Measuring Cup

Well-designed elements exceed the consumer's expectation. Consumers' appreciation to the product directly relates to brand loyalty which will extend the product experience. The "WOW" moment takes place when consumers engrave the image of the product and brand on their mind. The consumer experience is valuable and builds brand loyalty. The experience is a crucial reason consumer stay within the brand. In marketing, it is another significant moment when consumers show their loyalty to the brand they love. The personal product experience takes place through the Extend where designers should be thoughtful and considerate because the product engagement and its extension will yield consumer loyalty.

Millennials

Understanding target consumers and their characteristics frequently reveal important clues for a successful design. There are abundant consumer segments, and one of the most significant target consumers featuring its large size and unique characteristic is Generation-Y, better known as Millennials. Millennials are generally considered those born in the early 1980s to mid 1990s.
Millennials are also referred to as "Echo-Boomers" because they are the children of Baby-boomers.

42

Millennials are one of the largest groups to experience the digital and information revolution.[10]

Millennials live in the Information Age11, and they are comfortable in their usage of computer technology and multimedia. Millennials became mainstream adults in the 21st century, and they drive consumer behavior and directly impact the consumer market. It has been essential to understand and connect to them, and it is critical to foresee the path they are heading as they become the parents of Generation-Alpha, the first generation born entirely in the 21st century.

New Value

Unlike baby boomers who were striving to make a living for their family, their children, Millennials, faced the astonishing evolution of computers and digital media. They care less about social status, but more about real value and versatility. They do not consider owning property as a status symbol but treat it as the practical means by how to use it.

---

[10] The demographic cohort that is most often defined as individuals born between 1946 and 1964.

[11] Historic period beginning in the late 20th century and characterized by the rapid shift from traditional industry to information technology

They feel comfortable sharing living space, and accommodations such as Airbnb [12] become practical and widespread. Living space is transforming into the minimal and functional dwelling from a lifetime property to possess. As Uber [13] is reconciling the desires to own transportation, many millennials don't find a rationale to keep a car in the garage without using it. The new value proposition of Millennials own triggers new businesses catered to their demands, such as Airbnb and Uber, and we will continue see many more in years to come, as their generation matures and their needs change.

Sustainability

Green campaigns show alarming simulations of global warming and sea levels inundating cities. Revealing the limit of fossil fuel capacity triggers a need for alternative energy. As a result, a growing number of consumers are looking for renewable products that can offer secure and sustainable living.

---

[12] Online marketplace for arranging or offering lodging, primarily homestays, or tourism experiences.
[13] Multinational ride-hailing company offering services that include peer-to-peer ridesharing, ride service hailing, food delivery, and a micro mobility system.

Millennials are crusaders of the green movement. They are the frontier of using friendly shopping totes, saying goodbye to the plastic bags. They love hydro flask bottles, which the market forecasts to grow by approximately 4% in the next five years, replacing the PET (polyethylene terephthalate) materials which are not biodegradable. [14] Other examples include refillable liquid products, electric vehicles, reusable launch systems for Space X, and even a willingness to pay extra money for compostable food packaging. There will be many innovations derived from the sustainability movement.

Millennials are, without hesitation, adapting to the green movement, which is imperative to the survival of our species. They are motivated by connection in virtual communities. Social media such as Facebook, Pinterest, YouTube, and Instagram are growing astronomically by members generating content to share common interests to build continually growing green communities.

---

[14] Reusable Water Bottle Market Trends- Industry Analysis, Share, Growth, Product, Top Key Players and Forecast 2026

Healthy Lifestyle

As the new demand for a healthy lifestyle grows, the food industry shifts gears toward less processed and more nutritious food services for Millennials. Blue Apron[15] offers fresh vegetables and sustainable protein with a top-rated recipe for their young consumers to cook high-quality meals at home. As they face the negative impact of obesity, there are so many life-changing experiences offered to influence one another in the community.

For example, the Rock 'n' Roll [16] road running event offers a festive regional run in major US cities and is expanding the activities to Canada, Europe, China, and South America. During the pandemic of Covid-19, they promptly created virtual race events for the members to keep running while social distancing with other members.

Humanity

Technology massively impacts every facet of society. For example, more of our everyday

---

[15] Ingredient-and-recipe meal kit and easy to follow recipes services.

[16] The road running marathon series own by Ironman group

interactions are driven by personal electronic devices than by in-person dialogues. Are humans willing to accept virtual reality for romantic dating, or is analog space still necessary for humanizing contacts? Gerd Leonhard, the futurist, said that humanity will change more in the next 20 years than in the previous 300 years. [17] As the new generation is shaping our society, we are looking for ways that humanity can synchronize with technology.

In 2010, Apple released the iPhone 4 with the very first front-facing camera with Facetime, an application that enabled a video call. The second camera on the front side was not just an additional feature, but it delivered a story of humanity that connected friends and family. Since the advent of this technology, most smartphones offer the same functionality, which makes the investment meaningful. It is one way that a new idea and technology can create a product experience to reach humanity.

Involvement

---

[17] Technology vs. Humanity: The coming clash between man and machine

Millennials significantly influence the products and services that they use. This is in dramatic opposition to the behavior of previous generations. Millennials review and share product experiences proactively, and as a result, are often invited into the research focus groups in both physical and virtual spaces. They are willing to provide direct feedback and insight that can enhance the product experience in the future. It is a productive way to learn what they need and desire. The learnings are promising and likely lead to the success of the product and service.

In the information era, users' star ratings and reviews are other great examples of their involvement. From purchasing an expensive automobile to the everyday product, consumer reviews have never been so insightful. Those reviews and ratings are cumulating useful data for marketing teams to analyze and forecast for the market in the future. Utilizing the data is reliable as it is real-time information.

YouTube[18] creators, known as YouTubers, are just as diligent as the official product advertising for introducing new consumer electronics. YouTubers [19] are often commissioned to pre-experience the new product so that they can review and influence target groups. According to Tubics.com, there are 31 million YouTuber channels, uploading 500 hours of video every minute. The consumers' involvement in the digital space is fast and yields invaluable consumer insights. Those insights are considered relatively honest and accountable.

---

[18] Online video-sharing platform headquartered in San Bruno
[19] Individual(s) whose platform are YouTube channel, personalized subpages of the YouTube video sharing platform

2_DESIRE

"Design is the Education of Desire." [20]
-Kenya Hara

Henry Ford's famous invention in 1908 offered people a way to transport from one place to another. The need was clear, and Ford was convinced to proceed with mass production. Thus, the industrial revolution began; every consumer was happy to purchase the one iconic vehicle, the Model-T. When the factory's productivity gained efficiency, the production cost gradually decreased. After several years, though, consumers were not excited to see the same vehicle. So, Ford challenged themselves to appeal to consumer's desire for a more aesthetic design. It was one of the historical moments when American 'Industrial Design' was born.

---

[20] Kenya Hara, Designing design

Figure 4 Ford Model-A Coupe Advertising in 1930

Ford introduced the Model-A (Figure 4) to replace its predecessor. The Model-A was presented in October 1927 and was available to consumers after two months with an attractive burgundy exterior color and striking white rings on the wheels. The Model-A had triggered multiple models in the following years, and the transportation design era accelerated. Consumers brought their desired choice over the products, demanding preferences in addition to the functional benefit.

Today, consumers relentlessly desire products and services. In a massive market, their desires normally exceed functional needs when they are shopping for products and services. Today's consumer aspires to a product with an emotional aspect rather than just rational consuming.

Design has been a great contributor to this aspect in the market, and designers are encouraged to understand how they can offer products and service to fulfill consumers desires. There are many components and aspects from which designers can collectively utilize to understand consumers' minds. When the product meets a customer's appetite and is appealing enough to create a new attraction, it will sell and stay memorable. It is the moment where other significant components take place in between products and consumers. These are brand recognition, trust, and loyalty: the critical ingredients for the successful design. Once a consumer acknowledges the product and becomes loyal to the brand, they may stick to the brand until they find something better.

Pleasure

When customers are buying a product, they tend to look for a functional benefit first. But they are frequently hooked on a product not by a practical need, but by the pleasure.

An example from consumer research explains what pleasure means to the consumer. In Target retail stores, there was a decent upright vacuum cleaner that seemed powerful and reasonably priced, so Bethany (not a real name) decided to buy and try one. The vacuum cleaner functioned well, but it was a bit bulky and heavy to operate. Bethany felt vacuuming is an everyday chore that should be easy and enjoyable. After two years, she started to consider finding a lighter vacuum from a different brand. This time, Bethany chose one that was lightweight, easy to drive, and beautifully designed. She was fond of using the new product, and the fact that the product was compact and more comfortable to maneuver made her use it more often, not as a chore but a pleasure. As a result, Bethany decided to buy another product and suggested the product to her best friends and family.

The functionality will meet the consumer's desire for actual benefits. But the genuine opportunity extends to how the product can contribute to achieving the consumers' desire and produce pleasure. It is always worth looking at what types of pleasure a product development team can consider.

1. Physio-pleasure

People have multiple senses that can be triggered by elements that a product or service can offer. These senses can yield pleasure to consumers. The joy of the body: sights, sounds, smells, taste, and touch. Physio-pleasure combines many aspects of the visceral level with some of the behavioral level.[21] Most industrial design elements can enhance physio-pleasure both functionally and aesthetically by considering the product's form language and surface details.

2. Socio-pleasure

Social pleasure originates from interaction with others. Communication technologies such as smartphones, emails, texting, or even physical mail can play productive social roles.

For example, a coffee maker serves as a gathering point for ongoing social interactions in the office. Thus, socio-pleasure combines aspects of both behavioral and reflective design. Major coffee machine makers offer single-serve pod brewers, that provide a variety of samplers and fast service.

---

[21] Donald A. Norman, Emotional Design

It can attract a group of people to enjoy their coffee break without compromising their preferences and waiting time.

As our social trends move from personal value to inter-personal values, social aspects in product and service play a significant role that can encourage people to build stronger communities. It is a great place where design can contribute to the people who need a strong bond in a common interest.

3. Psycho-pleasure

This aspect of pleasure deals with people's reactions and psychological state during the use of products. Psycho-pleasure resides at the behavioral level. Thinking about a luxurious wine glass can complement the taste of wine and yield mental enjoyment.

Using a functional magnetic resonance imaging (fMRI) machine, researchers tried to measure if the price has a psychological association with the taste of wine. Researchers shared the prices of wines between $5 to $90 to the tasters, and discovered that tasters generated significantly higher spikes in the brain region that is associated with pleasure when they experience samples with a higher price tag.[22] The taste of the wine remains physically the same, but the perception of the value was enhanced as the user appreciates the product more.

4. Ideo-pleasure

Here lies the reflection on people's experiences. It is where one appreciates the aesthetics, or the quality of a product, for perhaps the extent to which a product enhances life and respects the environment. The value of many products comes from the statement they make. When exposed so that others can see them, the products provide ideo-pleasure to the extent that they signify the value judgments of their owner. Ideo-pleasure lies at the self-reflection. For example, an artistic product can recall an appreciation when he or she was young, and that personal memory can offer ideo-pleasure for life.

When I first saw the Ferrari Testarossa (Figure 5) in downtown Hong Kong, it

---

[22] 'Eager sellers and stony buyers, Understanding the psychology of new-product adoption' by John T. Gourville

appeared as a piece of beautiful sculpture compared to other automobiles of the same year. The engine had roared and drawn my full attention to it. The memory remains as an ideo-pleasure, and the red machine still marks as an all-time favorite car. I believe many people have similar ideo-pleasure moments in their mind. It is always interesting to figure out what triggers the ideo-pleasure.

Figure 5 Ferrari Testarossa F110, produced in 1996

Aspiration

Today's consumption happens from need, want, and desire. Consumers are seeing new products pop up every day. There are myriad new products in the market consumers have to choose from, and finding the right product is not an easy task. Smart consumers use data and don't mind some quick research if needed. Therefore, designers have to pay more attention to consumers aspirations. Product development should not be focusing on differentiating for a new look, but should focus on the voice from the consumer mind. Product success is directly related to the consumer aspirations and experiences that can be found or created, in many cases, by designers.

User Experience

While the experience journey map oversees the ecosystem around consumers, there is another tool that focuses explicitly on users' experience. This tool emphasizes a complete cycle of how users interact with the product. They call it 'User Experience 360' (Figure 6) as it makes a full circle view of user experience. It allows designers to look at how people interact with the product from a user's perspective. It is interesting to observe how users approach a product when they touch and interact with the functional and emotional elements. User Experience 360 helps to illustrate the cycle that users repeat. This tool specifies the users' experience and interaction in a physical and a mental layer where they try to get functional and emotional benefits.

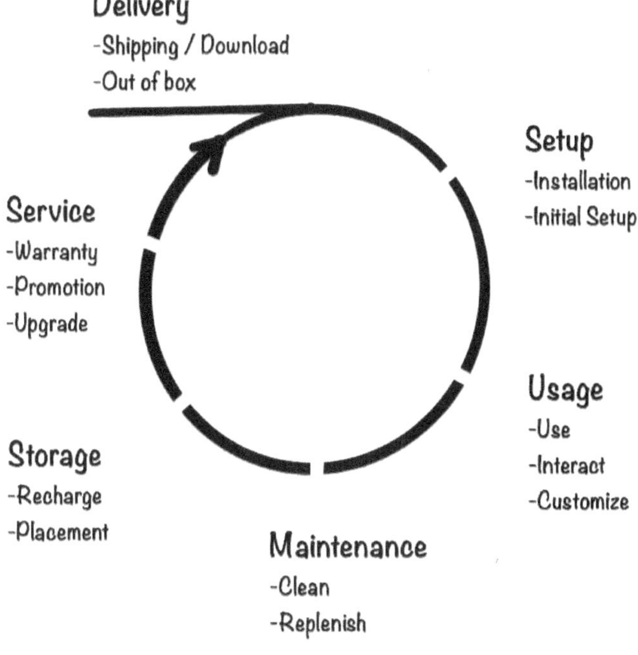

Figure 6 User Experience 360

Unlike buying experience, User experience 360 provides designers with functional and emotional values that directly connect to users. As a result, the relationship between the user and product can occur, and the practical and emotional interface can improve together on an aspirational level.

Seduction

The seductive power of design in specific forms and materials can transcend issues of price and safety. What alluring products have in common is their ability to create a strong emotional bond with their customers, almost like desperation.[23]

The seduction may appeal to the market for a while, but is this model sustainable? Every product has a lifetime and cannot last forever. In other words, designers can consider how the product seduces the consumer to offer valued experience and make an impression during the product lifetime. It is somehow related to industry ethics to take into consideration.

---

[23] Donald A. Norman, Emotional Design, why we love (or hate) everyday things

Design ethics has been an issue for vaping products that have appealed to underaged consumers. The products are as attractive as fashion accessories and can mislead teenagers into nicotine addiction. There is no hard rule for design ethics. However, when designers create something, they ask two questions for ethical measure. "Does this design care for the users and make their life better?" If designers can find the right answers, that is a sign of sustainable success.

Loyalty

What do customers associate with a ketchup bottle? There are a handful of design elements that people unconsciously identify with their favorite condiments. Creating a bottle design is the result of many factors, from complicated manufacturing restrictions to everyday usage.

Heinz, as an example, delivers the product to both homes and restaurants. The design of bottles in general has been evolving for centuries, and the value for the bottle design has been instrumental.[24] In addition to being served alongside delicious food, the legendary faceted bottle design with a crown

---

[24] Kraft Heinz Company

label proudly placed along the long neck is streamlined. When these elements collaboratively work together over time, they become a recognizable signature that represents the brand. The signature image is a considerably valuable asset for the company because it connects to their consumers. In the best practice, the signature elements function as the brand DNA. For loyal consumers, the signature can recall what they have experienced in the past and reassure the continuing engagement with the brand. For new consumers, a unique product experience begins with a signature that can attract and engage over time.

1. Signature

For the new ketchup bottle design development[25], the design team looked at all the Heinz bottles in history. The team realized the faceted bottle surface detail and the crown label are the significantly valuable elements that must carry over to the new design. Designers were encouraged to pay attention to the signature elements because it may be barely recognized, and not perceived as a critical element.

---

[25] Ziba was commissioned to design a next generation of the iconic Heinz ketchup bottle

The design team came up with a contemporary silhouette featuring the new bottle design, working relentlessly to get the right proportion and the specific volume requirements for the bottle. Hundreds of prototypes were milled on the CNC machine to find out the best aesthetics and maintain the brand image and while appealing to the new consumers. Out of the countless Styrofoam models, the team hand-selected the final bottle design and meticulously sculpted and detailed the signature elements: the prestigious facets and crown label. While it was challenging to make the signature elements perceivable, it was a valuable and rewarding design practice for the team to carry over the brand's heritage and awareness. (Figure 7)

Figure 7 Heinz the original bottle (on life) design in 1906 vs. the new bottle (on right) design in 2016

2. Brand Loyalty

The condiment that has been gracing dinner tables for centuries must have carried a secret quality to survive in the fastidious consumer market. It is amazing to see one generation who loves a product carry over the family choice of condiments to their children as a tradition. It is an excellent example of brand royalty.

Out of millions of products in the market, a fraction of products may be privileged to stand for brand loyalty from their consumers. One of the factors contributing to brand loyalty is where the brand's signature element resides. In the best application, the brand's signature image relentlessly resonates with a memorable icon that the consumers perceive, remember, and hand over to others.

Brand loyalty seems more powerful than ever today. Frequently, customers become involved with product development by participating in the brand's consumer research. Word of mouth always impacts the product and service in favor of the brand. The consumer rating in the virtual retail space is a significant phenomenon where loyal customers trigger first-time consumers. At most, it is sturdy and practical marketing for no cost.

03_EGO TO ECO

'As we see the divisions that the last few generations have painstakingly erected out of similar statistics, we find no need for more such distinct areas but unity. Not the specialist, but the synthesis is required.' [26]
-Victor Papanek

Social Design

Industries that have developed themselves amid highly competitive markets stay strong on what they are good at. To adopt a new market, they need to reiterate how the product and service can retain existing customers and reach out to new people. That is why product development should be rooted in a specific consumer group, a "target market" in other words. The development team and consumers

---

[26] The Green Imperative, Natural design for the real world, by Victor Papanek

organically share resources and information to develop products' core competencies for the sake of a better product.

Future industries and their technologies will need to focus on how to make the market ecosystem sustainable, especially between the product provider and consumers. During the Covid-19 outbreak in 2020, people stayed home to decrease spread of the virus. Zoom[27], the video communication service, was one of the most excellent products that contributed to bringing people back together. Through online meeting applications, schools initiated distance learning from small to a large group. Products like a social media apps are, in the long run, the way to shape the future from Ego to Eco.

Retro-Social

People look back and learn from their mistakes in history. Architects build houses based on failures in the past, making future buildings safer and more reliable. Looking back always gives developers lessons and provides more opportunities for future product development. Thus, we build up better products and services. This is a great way to

---

[27] Enterprise video communications, with an easy, reliable cloud platform for video and audio conferencing.

communicate with designers who have come before us. The closer we look at the past challenges and achievements, the more we can learn to build a better future.[28]

Retro-social has never been easier. Pinterest boards can be a great source of universal design that has been used by product developers. They can collect and sort abundant images and references in a reasonably short time. This exercise can nourish the team's creativity, and this is always productive.

Form & Formless

"In the Industrial Age, when they tried to master aspects of form, a return to the content is already overdue."
-Victor Papanek

The statement above sounds dated, and we are already living in an all-new era. The market is inundated with digital content. The size of the industry is unmeasurable, and audiences continuously demand more.

The formless products such as communication subscription service, cloud service for data storage,

---

[28] Henry Petroski, The evolution of useful things

and streaming media are maturing. This indicates how designers can remaster the aspects of new design accordingly, for both form and formless products. In the digital content-heavy industry, designers naturally focus more on digital products. It is uncertain how designers can create a shapeless design that provides visual guidance for consumers to access the hardware and physical services.

Thus, designers should be encouraged to integrate the form and formless product for the best product experience. It is not the best idea to specialize in hardware and software separately and incorporate them with a third party. Because in the worst case, it turns out to be Frankenstein. We will talk about how to combine the software and the hardware to create the best consumer experience on 07_ EXPERIENCE Humanity.

04_EMPATHY

People frequently suffer from discomfort and difficulty in approaching commodities in everyday life. A badly designed computer mouse can cause carpal tunnel syndrome and illegible signage can mislead people in transit. Carelessly designed products cause frustration and distress. Over time, the disengagement between products and users builds up a feeling of discomfort and distrust in consumers' minds. This unpleasant product experience can negate the product image and its brand.

Designers are encouraged to look at negative experiences so that they can identify the pain points. Empathy is an excellent tool for doing so. When designers develop a product for consumers whom they have not met before, they can go out to see the consumers and witness the real pains on site. Designers occasionally feel empathy for people who suffer from a specific difficulty and are motivated to find the right solution. It is a crucial moment where designers can create great ideas to resolve a particular problem. Empathy is one of the most powerful ways to fulfill product development for goodwill.

Compassion

While the strategies are practical, design compassion can help to approach the consumer differently. Compassionate design is a deep concern for the consumers' sufferings and misfortunes. Many products are not considered thoroughly enough and result in wasted resources and disappointment. Design compassion can be a powerful tool in many ways to develop products that are genuinely purposeful and well-considered to fit the consumers' life. Design compassion is one of the key ingredients for Design Recipe.

During product development, the designer and consumer can be the same person, or they can be two completely different people. If designers can find compassion and empathize with the target consumers and the issues, the product solution can be found quickly. If they cannot, it may show a disconnect.

There are a few examples of design compassion. Designers who ever experienced vision disabilities will best understand the difficulty of listening to a critical time being announced in a crowded train station. This inspired the braille watch design. (Figure 8)

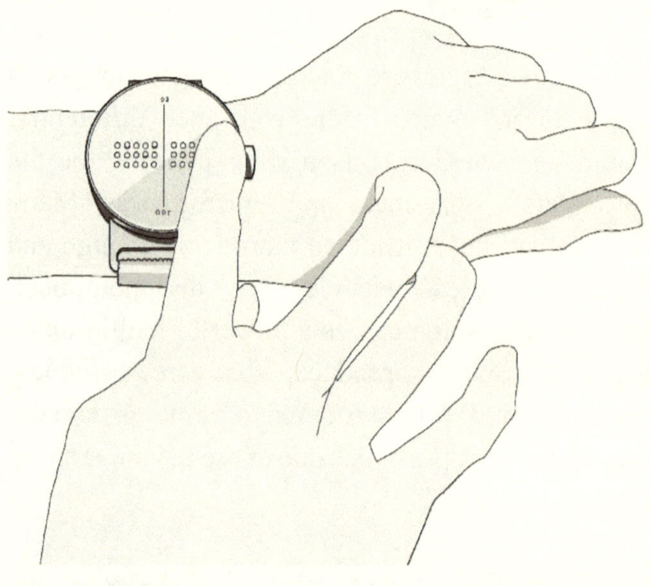

Figure 8 DOT Watch: aims to make the visually impaired get the necessary information more easily.

The designers who are enthusiastic about outdoor sports will best understand the POV (point of view) action video camera and its use capturing exciting moments to share in their community.

Despite this, designers do not have to be blind nor a sports enthusiast to be compassionate about their jobs. Design compassion is a mindset. The designer's mind can be motivated by empathy to understand the target consumers' desperate needs. It is goodwill to design better products just like you do it for your friends and family. A compassionate designer can connect with consumers in many different ways. With the interpersonal connection to consumers, designers are motivated to pull out what is truly needed to improve experiences and add value for consumers.

A commercial for Nasake, a sake from Fukushima, Japan, said that 'compassion' has the power to move others.[29] Compassionate design approaches may not be recognizable in a short time, but the consideration can be found and remembered in users' minds throughout the product experience. What is astonishing is that compassionate design, in the long run, can significantly improve brand awareness and build invaluable customer loyalty.

---

[29] NASAKE - Fukushima Sake Story
WEB ： http://fukushima-sake.com

Curiosity

One suggested way to practice empathy is putting the designer's feet into the consumer's shoes. It is a great way to consider consumers' minds. Every consumer is different, and it can be difficult to become who they are. It is a mindset of designers that brings questions of who the users are and curiosities of where they would suffer deep in their minds. The curiosity can help to observe our target consumers reasonably well and is always instrumental. If designers are not the target consumer, and there is no curiosity involved during product development, the result will have difficulty surviving in the market.

Care

Successful designs last, reaching to the soul and serving desperate needs. Successful design cares about the users personally, and thus generates a positive impression. We are facing so many products in the care categories, such as beauty-care, skin-care, oral-care, fem-care, water-care, air-care, fabric-care, and more. Taking care of consumers is another key ingredient to success. When the benefit reaches the depths of consumers' needs, they come back and share the pride of the possession.

| REMEMBER & USE |

The consumer journey can be defined by Looking at the user's persona and their experience with products. Emotional design and its implementation will earn loyalty from consumers like Millennials.

Understanding consumers' pleasure (physio, socio, psycho, and ideo) will aid in the development of the product concept, and allow the team to understand their aspiration. Landing on the desired concept will lead to loyalty from consumers.

By embracing the peer to peer community and practicing social and retro social designs, the team, whether the product has form or is formless, should be able to adopt the changes in the market.

A compassionate approach to consumers will open up the team's vision. Curiosity and care are excellent tools for empathetic approaches.

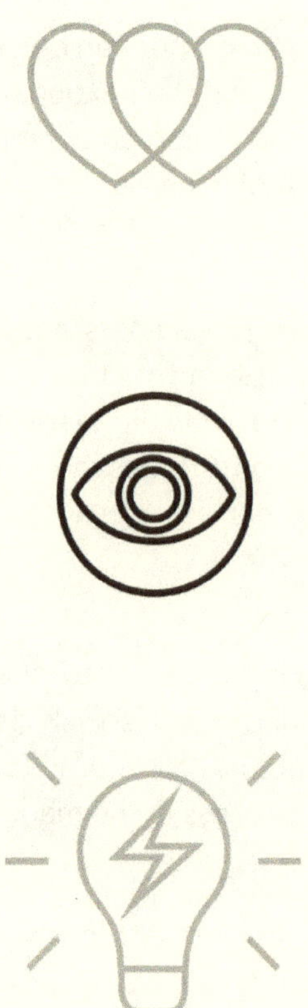

| PART 2 |

FOCUS
QUALITY

*"Design activity is not for a difference,
but the difference is a consequence of
a great design."*
*-The genius behind Apple's greatest
products*

Part 2: FOCUS

05_PURPOSE

Rationale

Developing a profitable product takes significant resources and dedication. The amount of investment in design development equals the level of design quality the product will deliver. However, the equation may not work as planned unless the development team articulates the design rationale. A creative process typically does not have a hard rule to follow and is frequently biased by unnecessary elements that distract designers from focusing on critical problems.

As I mentioned in Part 1, designers need to understand the product's backgrounds: consumer, brand, and social trends. Then they ideate multiple designs from the learnings and verify the design concepts with engineers and the marketing team to choose the final design concept. As the product development team manipulates the design process to create a great product that resonates with the target consumers, designers are strongly encouraged to focus on two parts: the functional and emotional designs.

1. Functional Design

Products and services are selling in the consumer market, primarily for the functional benefits that serve people. The functionality is often intuitively recognized and works effortlessly. The practical benefits are what consumers look for, thus highly expected to fulfill. Most likely, lack of or weak practicality and functional benefit results in a product that will fail in the market.

The traditional product with pure functionality often appears industrial and primitive. The hammer, for example, was designed purely for practical reasons, and the paper clip was invented for nothing but holding papers. It is what we traditionally refer to with the phrase: Form follows function. Functional designs encourage designers and engineers to collaborate for specific practical benefits. In the sequence of product development, MVP (minimum viable product)[30] can be a good example that requires an only functional design to appeal to early consumers and provide feedback for future product development.

2. Emotional Design

In addition to the functional design, there are unique design elements that make the product emotionally connect to the consumers. These elements are usually built together with function features, and emotional design elements are likely related to the psychological benefits. The emotional benefits feature what consumers desire to fulfill their inner needs.

Emotional product design can be as simple as an emoticon on the smartphone screen, but the element can powerfully touch people's minds. It opens up significant design opportunities in addition to what a functional product can offer. For the most part, an explicitly articulated design language can create emotional design elements. As the language arts can express human emotion,

---

[30] A version of a product with just enough features to satisfy early customers and provide feedback for future product development.

the design language and its beautiful image can develop the product and service that resonates with consumers' emotional needs and desires. The design language is often firmly related to the brand, which 09_SERVICE Brand Equity will cover.

Emotional design can develop in a couple of different ways. For example, Honda[31] uses multiple key fobs for a family minivan. Each key remembers a seat setting for individual users. When one of the family members approaches the door, the seat will automatically adjust the customized position before the driver gets in. It is an example of design creating a personal connection, in addition to functional features, which bring the user experience to the next level. Emotional design can work by aesthetic design elements that draw visual attention to the product at an attraction level. Product surface details such as color, material, and finish are often useful for emotional design.

For example, the Toyota Rav4 hybrid model offers 17 color options from a traditional

---

[31] Honda Motor Company, Ltd. is a Japanese public multinational conglomerate corporation primarily known as a manufacturer of automobiles

metallic white to the contemporary two-tone colors from which customers can customize. Emotional design opportunity is as broad as designers' creative imagination. Because human emotion can work best in person, the emotional design effort should be articulated and contemplated based on the profound understanding of human behaviors. When the product service touches a consumer, the result will be rewarded by the design team and the company's brand. As many small-sized companies are starting up their business these days, emotional design elements will help their product and service to be viable in the market.

Success

These days, society relentlessly offers products and services. They are fulfilling needs on one end or leaving consumers with frustration on the other end. We, on the part of consumers, must be diligent in finding out what is the right product that meets our needs. Successful design not only interacts with users, but it lasts to extend the product experience. Happy consumers make an influence on market trends and share positive experiences for other people to join. Product success always comes from people. Thus, product designers are always encouraged to identify who they are.

Survival of the fittest

As consumers are making a transition from one generation after another, their needs and desires are evolving. As Charles Darwin[32] quoted in his book, On the origin of species, it is not the strongest nor intelligent that survives, but the one most responsive to change. As Darwin's origin of species assimilates to change, the successful design is not the one the strongest visual attraction of its kind that survives, nor the most intellectual, but the most responsive to change to adapt to the new consumers.

Strategy

Successful design and service require an excellent strategy. A strategic design consists of three things: how to meet consumer needs, how to manufacture, and how to sell. All three are individually essential and do not negotiate with one another to make the

---

[32] Geologist and biologist, best known for his contributions to the science of evolution

product successful. Because every consumer product has one common goal, profitability, a purposeful strategic plan will be essential to be successful by all means: desirability (for the consumer), feasibility (for production), and viability (for business). (Figure 9)

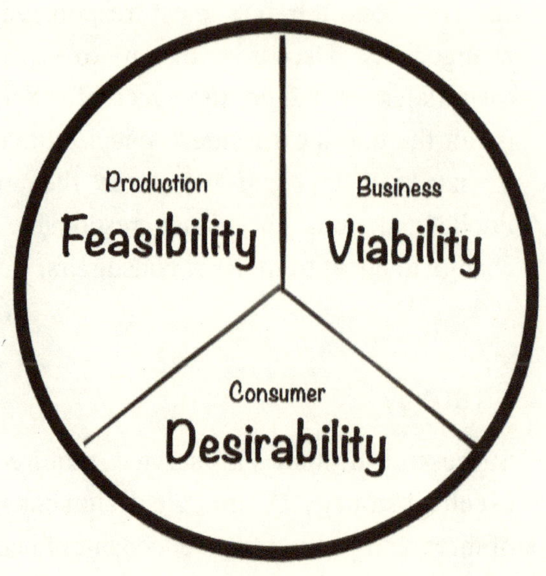

Figure 9 Successful Product Development Strategy

06_PROBLEM

The productive design process is subjective. Some design teams work as an independent team, while others belong to a bigger group that includes engineering and operations teams. The creative process also works differently depending on the team members and their cultures. An aggressive schedule is a typical hurdle that designers must overcome. Design teams usually have a preferred way of working that reflects the team culture. Creative design work consistently requires the group dynamic, which motivates them to collaborate with others. The team power varies depending on who the members and the target consumers are.

In a prominent organization, the design team may experience communication barriers and misalignments with other groups. These are typical distractors that keep designers away from focusing on the core problem. In this case, how can a design team maintain the creative jobs and meet an aggressive deadline? Is there a tool to generate innovative and creative design concepts?

Creative Force

When designers enter the concept exploration phase, they frequently see limited resources and time. As the team is heading to the concept refinement phase, designers must make sure the concepts are strong enough to make a firm alignment with teams.

By all means, helping the design team focus on core problems and improve the quality of the product experience is not negotiable. The following items contribute to the 'Creative Force' that can help designers focus on the core design problems and generate bulletproof design concepts consistently so that the team can move forward.

Focus

At the 1997 Apple Worldwide Developers Conference, Steve Jobs shared this brilliant piece of advice: "Focusing is about saying no. It isn't easy, but the payoff can be quite rewarding." As Jobs said, "I'm actually as proud of the things we haven't done as the things I have done." We may think that the CEO juggled a number of projects at once to reach success. But he credited much of his success to one word: Focus.

The Creative force on product development starts from ruling out what is not relevant so that creative energy can focus on the essence of the problem to solve. The focus will function better if the core problem is isolated from the secondary ones. It is important to keep multiple issues resolved at the same time if it is doable. However, the designer must prioritize the core problem and focus on that, so that the product can meet what consumers desire the most.

Function

Design activity must be functional. There should be a right answer for everything designers do. Useful products can give a good reason for what the product means to the users. As I mentioned in 05_PURPOSE Rational, designers should approach the function in two distinctive ways: practical and emotional.

For example, I once worked on a team which had a contract for a tableware company called Libbey. Our team was helping Libbey to develop a line of serving plates for Millennials. Our design team has learned that the target consumers love parties and are fond of multi-purpose partywares that fit well in an urban lifestyle.

Through multiple concept reviews, the design team came up with unique plate designs that feature dual-face serving tray. In addition to that, a modular wood insert can be removed from the main tray base to function in multiple ways.

As the practical purpose was focused on the consumers' needs, the design team focused on emotional use, as the concept was strategically telling the urban story. The team had gone through brainstorms to generate abundant sketch concepts for the form language and explored in search of the right materials.

Interestingly, the design team found that Millennials prefer authentic materials to synthetic ones. Target consumers do not value glass-like plastic or wood-like synthetic material. They emotionally love authentic quality and experience. Through selection of materials verified with food safety and production feasibility, the design team specified the beautiful ceramic and scratch-resistant acacia wood that forms a modern hexagon design. The final design successfully reflects the unique characteristics of Millennials. (Figure 10)

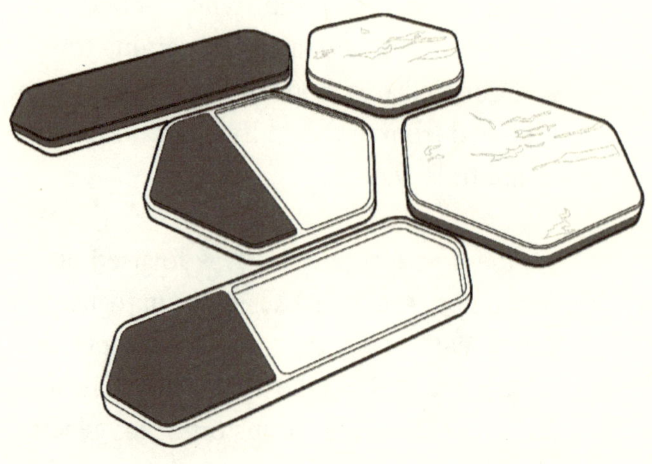

Figure 10 Libbey Urban Story Serving Plate Set

Simplicity

If the design team needs a universal rule that will fit every consumer, this is the rule: "Have nothing in your design that you do not know to be useful, or believe to be beautiful."[33] The law of simplicity will safely guide designers into the most minimal solution possible. The great designers use the rule of simplicity, which is a great way to minimize visual noise. As Kenya Hara[34] said, "Objects that are made simply may first appear monotonous. However, in their accumulations of calmly determined design choices are discovered the invisible comfort of daily life."

Simplicity can alternatively mean 'appropriate complexity.' To ordinary people, the cockpit of an aircraft may look surprisingly complicated and hard to understand. But that is not the case for the pilots: to them, the instruments are all logical, and thoughtfully organized into a functional group. In complex product development, simplicity may not be easily achievable. A simple design should be the result of understanding the complexity of a product.

---

[33] William Moris, A British texile designer, poet, novelist
[34] Kenya Hara, the art director of MUJI

For the simplest design solution, designers must be able to prioritize the functional layers of products. The core of design practice is to achieve simplicity as a result.

Striving for simplicity is not an easy task. It is always harder to create simple solutions than complex ones. Because complex product experience often yields confusion and misleads consumers, designers should always exercise constraint to conclude the most straightforward design solution. As pointed out, the accumulation of simple solutions will serve the invisible comfort and the room to spare. And as a result, the user can focus more on the valuable attributes.

Balance

By definition, Balance is the visual weight of elements in a composition. The distinctive design element is relatively well appreciated when it delivers in the right balance with others. Designers consider the balance of proportions such as forms, details, and spaces. It is also important to keep hard against soft and simple against dynamic. Too much of one thing causes unnecessary attention that feels off-balance, which could also be useful to create dynamism when needed. Whether it visually draws attention or disappears in a composition, it is all depending on the designer's intent. A well-arranged design element is aesthetically pleasing. Particularly balanced parts fulfill a purpose or achieve a targeted look and feel. Success in manipulating design elements in the right balance can help to make an aesthetically outstanding design.

ET66 (Figure 11) is a great example that illustrates a perfect balance that esthetically appeals to many users. As individual elements are balanced, the similar parts can be clustered in a functional group and practically balanced with the other group. In the UX/UI interface design, the primary group of buttons can visually balance with the secondary keys. Without the cluster and considerate balance, the interface can result in an unpleasant and complicated user experience.

Figure 11   Braun Calculator ET66 in 1981

When the functional and emotional design elements orchestrate together to resonate with a single unified image, the product can offer a harmonious and beautiful service. It's like a symphony in which distinctive musical instruments make a harmonic sound that creates a delightful experience for the audience.

Accent

An accent can be a fun part that highlights a small visual detail such as color, material, and finish. The micro visual elements can quietly draw attention and function.

Richard Sapper is one of the most influential designers known for using visual accents that create surprise. His legendary Tizio lamp (Figure 12), for example, uses a visual accent in the functional joints. The small accents in the bright red color make the overall desk lamp whimsical and lively. The traditional desktop lighting has been selling since 1972.

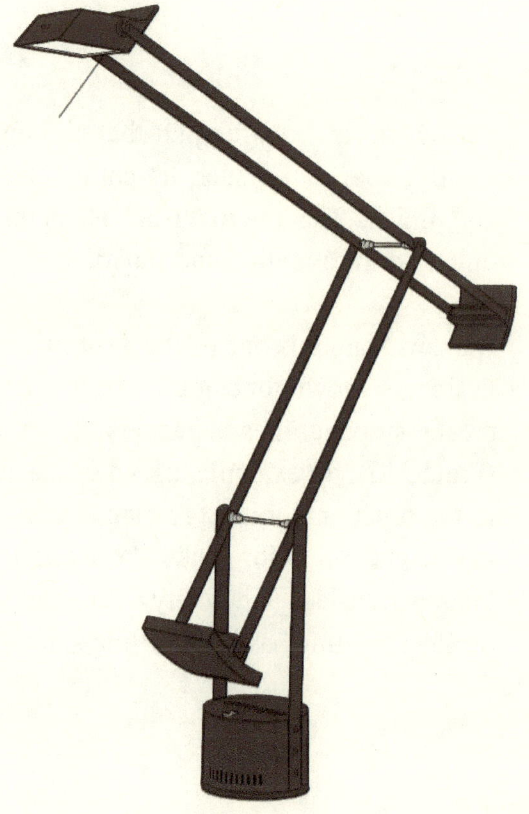

Figure 12 Tizio Table Lamp Designed by Richard Sapper in 1972

In a simple and minimal design language, designers can find a place to apply an accent element to indicate users' interaction points. The small detail can effectively draw attention for users to intuitively interact with the functional benefits. Another example resides in the Trackpoint at the center of Lenovo ThinkPad keypad. The bright orange color appears as a significant graphical accent and works as a pointing stick, substituting as a mouse when the computer is being used portably. For ThinkPad, this accent element became the signature element that ties up all product lines as one family. Even though the accent is functionally polarizing, it works as a brand DNA that consumers recognize and remember. As I will highlight again in 09_SERVICE Brand Equity, the emphasis can be an excellent tool for creating brand recognition.

Details

"God is in the details"[35] is an idiom that is expressing the idea that whatever one does should be completed in-depth because details are significantly crucial for the quality product. Barcelona Chair is one of the most renowned pieces that depicted the structural simplicity and meticulous craftmanship. (Figure 12) Similarly, "The devil is in the detail" refers to a catch or undefined element hidden in the details, meaning that something might seem simple at a first look but will take more time and effort to finalize than expected.

---

[35] Ludwig Mies van der Rohe, German-born architect by *The New York Times*

Figure 13 Barcelona Chair Designed by Ludwig Mies van der Rohe

The product development team uses a bulk of time and effort to initiate and develop a product. They call it "exploration and refinement". The exploration phase is fast, and the team sees the visual progression and evolution of the product. Once the product turns into a form, the core team remains to focus on details. The detailing may take an unpredictably long time and solitary dedication. During this time, designers can get involved in elevating the quality of the product. Otherwise, the devil can hide the undefined details that will impact the product quality.

When the product's primitive form requires mechanical design, everything else is considered details. Unlike primary form language that is immediately recognizable, the details appear and work during the product experience. They are the key elements that approach the consumer's emotions over time. As a result, excellent details can lead to an opportunity that can contribute to a quality product.

Every detail has a design challenge within itself, and attention paid to small things has big rewards. Thus, designers should treat details carefully, not inadvertently. It is no exaggeration to say that thoughts must be granted to every minute detail: parting lines, the radius around corners, the feeling of texture, the color, the graphics, and everything else.

Visualization

Great design requires collaborative efforts. Design development should concurrently work with hardware and software teams regularly to fulfill the functional and emotional purpose. The team creates primary form and adds the nitty-gritty product details, including color, finish, and material. The design team still needs a few more jobs to provide the final visualization: graphics, brands, logistic labels, and package.

Sooner or later, the design team comprehends preliminary design works and unique details and is rendering the final product design. Graphical assets can present in the latter part of the process. The visualization will encourage the whole team to align to a significant business decision. This visualization is typically demonstrated in a computer rendering. The design team can also consider using the three-dimensional prototype for the extended team to review the design concept before it is handed over to the production phase.

Every design process is different, and each product has its priority. The visualization will still be one of the most critical roles the design team can provide. The design team is always encouraged to visualize from the early ideation by hand sketch to the full-scale model by the 3D prototype.

Context

There is no good or bad design. In the ideal design field, there is only the right design. The design should always be created, analyzed, and evaluated in the context of the consumer and business needs. The design concepts should derive from the relevant context, but not from arbitrary places. To prioritize in context, designers should be working first for the consumer, then the stakeholder, and then for themselves.

A well-managed context brings more business opportunities for great works. Designers are frequently asked by the audience, "What is your favorite concept?" The answer should be well-balanced between the designer's ego and what is right for the success of the design. Context is also crucial in how the product is related to its surrounding. Great architecture enhances its value when it resonates with the land and atmosphere around it.

Originality

"An original writer is not one who imitates nobody, but one whom nobody can imitate." [36]

- René de Chateaubriand

It is necessary to ignore style and instead search for the originality of an object, its true nature. To find the Originality of object, designers must venture to its depth, through a rigorous design process, discarding all superfluous and superficial aspects. This design process is well illustrated by a story about a famed Indian carver of elephants. When asked how such beautiful elephants were carved, and he simply replied – "Oh! It's quite simple. I get a piece of wood and remove everything that is not an elephant!"

Originality usually derives from focusing on core problems. It takes time and dedication to identify those issues. Therefore, designers are always encouraged to put users at the center

---

[36] French writer, François-René de Chateaubriand

of purposeful experiences. This focus on the user enables designers to create a unique and original product. The design originality is a valuable asset that belongs to the design team. As we are facing the information era, originality is easily referred to by other designers. Design Recipe will cover how to protect the original design on 13_BUSINESS Intellectual Property.

07_HUMANITY

When the iPhone 4 introduced Facetime in 2010, the 90-second advertising clip did not point out any sign of technology about the new phone they released that day. The ad solely presents heartwarming stories with the legendary jazz vocal of Louis Armstrong[37] singing "When you're smiling, the whole world smiles with you." The ad streamed: "A baby is smiling at dad, who seems to be traveling far from home. A girl in her college graduation is smiling to grandparents who could not come. And a pregnant lady and her baby seen in ultrasonic vision are smiling to the proud dad on duty in Afghanistan."

The live motion pictures transmitted the emotional expression through a smart device to the friend and family. Viewers were fascinated not because it was

---

[37] American trumpeter, composer, vocalist, and actor who was among the most influential figures in jazz

possible by the latest front-facing camera and revolutionary video telephony technology, but instead, it was a humanizing experience that is sharing real-life emotion.

Who is Human?

Humans are socially interacting, learning and evolving from and using artifacts. Unlike other creatures, humans are intentional about socializing, throwing parties and planning events. We even create a community or legal structure to ensure that our social activity is sustainable. It is only humans who are skilled teachers at educating, analyzing, and formalizing data for our needs. Humans are the only creature dealing with complex and cognitive artifacts that require specialized skills and materials.

Intellect

Humans possess a highly developed intellect, the power of reasoning and understanding objectively, especially concerning abstract or academic matters. This intellectual property allows humans to explore art, games, humor, language, music, ritual, storytelling, and ultimately the appreciation of beauty.[38] These are the gifts that humans are always fond of, enjoy, appreciate, and love. They often dedicate themselves to pursue those gifts and say doing so is a reason for living. Reflecting on those gifts and target consumers allows designers to start the humanizing design story. As product designers create user's intellectual experience, the design will deliver a quality product service, and consumers will happily join.

Play

Designers can humanize their products with playful and creative ideas. A playful design element can render products approachable, and as a designer, it is fun utilizing design elements such as color, form, graphics, and details. There are no rules that medical products or professional instruments should not be fun. As medical devices are transforming into the life science product categories, designers can disrupt the stigmatic medical image with an approachable design that is friendly to use. For example, ECG (Electrocardiogram) device used to be an institutional device to test for heart defects, but it now also serves for monitoring heart activities to enhance athletic performance.

---

[38] Things that make us smart, by Donald A. Norman

Playful design elements make a product enjoyable beyond its functionality. It helps users engage with the product and use it better and more. Lorenz Static[39], the tabletop clock, is one of the greatest examples. The clock wittily faces the user as it awkwardly lays unbalanced. The half-capsule form factor keeps the design in a manipulated viewing angle while the base barely touches the tabletop giving a user no clue how the product can stay balanced without falling. The Static clock is embedded with a weight inside at the bottom point, so it is physically stable while it looks unbalanced. It stands up spontaneously when pushed over, which users frequently do for fun. Richard Sapper, as one of the most important industrial designers of his generation, was commissioned to design Lorenz Static clock in his early years, and acclaimed that the elements of wit and surprise will inspire a humanizing product experience. (Figure 14)

---

[39] Lorenz Static, a desktop clock designed by Richard Sapper

Figure 14 Lorenz Static Clock designed by Richard Sapper in 1960

08_VALUE

Design Value

All design activities must add value. A design value is not something to find, but something to create. To do that, designers must focus on the intrinsic value and make it viable and creditable.

I was a junior designer at Samsung in the 2000s. There was an unexpected concept development project for which our design team had to deal with buyers from Sun-Microsystem. Our team was preparing several TFT-LED monitor concepts so that the buyers could choose the final product. The Sun Microsystem team and our Marketing team asked my design team to propose the design concept renderings without an appropriate design process. Therefore, our work proceeded as a marketing sales force with which the team simply made an OEM (original equipment manufacturer) deal. The value of design jobs was not super clear, nor was the motivation. Thus, my design team didn't get acknowledged, but the Marketing team got the credit. My design team could have used the high 'creative force' if they had treated the design proposal as valuable work. The sale event went well as a collaborative effort made an OEM deal successfully. However, the moment has remained with me for many years, causing me to reflect on how the design effort can build a significant value with high design force that is measurable and creditable.

Intrinsic Value

Intrinsic value refers to an organization's value proposition of design, such as corporate image, product perception, brand identity, and the overall product service. Acknowledging the product's intrinsic value is extremely important for team leaders who are responsible for the success of the product. Managing the inherent value of design can be subjective and hard to measure. However, all designers should be encouraged to develop intrinsic values along with the development team.

When the team unanimously agrees and loves a design concept, there is a greater chance that the product the same reaction from the consumers. A successful idea often makes the team excited and brings dynamic energy and morale in the studio. Many design teams focus on creating 'WOW' concepts, and designers work hard to elevate the design concepts until the end of the development. Most importantly, consistent quality designs will enhance the company's brand value.

Designers should create product elements the way consumers like to be perceived emotionally and physically. It means that designers must comprehensively deal with physical, mental, and social aspects. During the product experience journey, which I mentioned on 05_PURPOSE Rationale, consumers consider how a product works physically and emotionally, as well as how it reflects their lifestyle to their friends and families.

When the design resonates with the brand messages and helps consumers perceive a valuable experience, we believe the design possesses intrinsic value for the consumers. The inherent design value of a product can grow in the market and proudly build significant benefits for the brand. A valuable design can impact a customer's everyday life and leverage the brand perception, which will in return be an invaluable asset for the organization.

The role of product design has been evolving. Traditionally, it was an afterthought of product development. The engineering team worked on parts and circuit boards with all the components laid out, and then designers put housing on top. The traditional process lacked collaboration between engineers and designers. For example, commercial product manufacturers, such as the medical industry, still think of design work as the A-surface[40] that covers the front-facing side of a product. As the industry grows and design is seen as a significant part of business, design teams often take responsibility to assert the role of design as a crucial part of the business. Therefore, designers are strongly encouraged to build design principles as intellectual guidelines.

The design principle should be able to identify the brand and create the appropriate design language for an individual product. For large corporations, they go beyond and

---

[40] The term is most generally used, is the outermost or uppermost layer of a physical object or space. It is the portion or region of the object that can first be perceived by an observer using the senses of sight and touch.

establish not only the product design but build the corporate design language, which unifies the company image.

So, what does Design Language stand for, and what are the actionable tools to support the design principles?

Design Language

The design of products and services utilizes the visual language. The visual vocabulary consists of aesthetic elements that can be perceived by consumers. The visual element delivers aesthetic values that are significant to consumers. As more and more product designs develop, it has been critical that the design language is discretely planned and executed. (Figure 15)

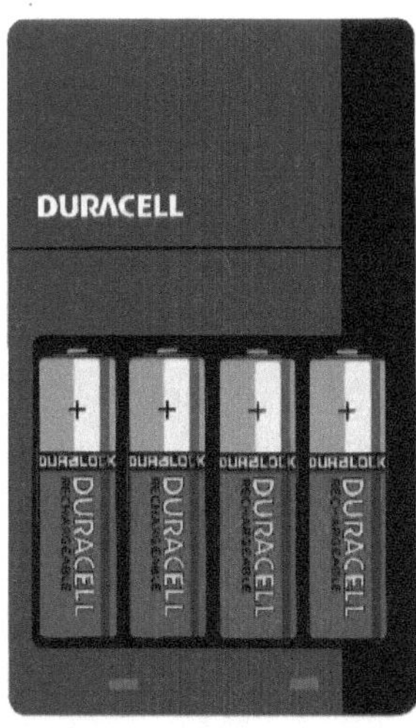

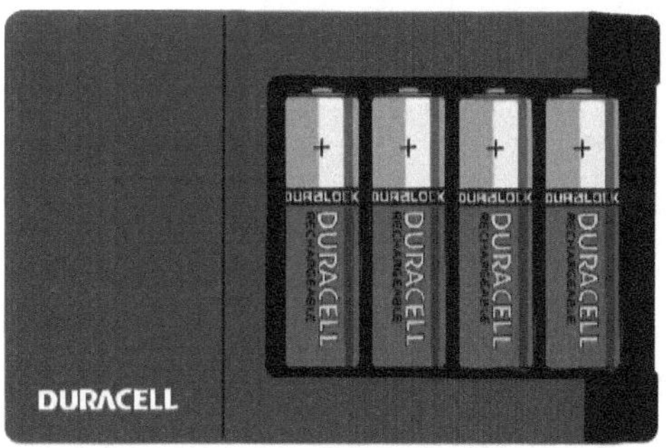

Figure 15 Duracell CEF Battery Charger DL

Design principles formulate the products' visual elements, and designers share the product design intents with the leadership, marketing, and engineering teams. Design principles work as a visual guideline for all the product lines. For example, outdoor products use dynamic and durable design language whereas indoor products convey friendly and simple images that blend into a home environment. By setting up a visual design language, the organization can train how the product design and service intends to appeal to its consumers.

The core design language will simplify products' design and help designers to minimize unnecessary visual elements under the single guideline.

1. VDL

VDL (Visual Design Language) is pervasively useful in corporations and design agencies. VDL is about understanding strategic brands and target consumers and yielding the design attributes to create the visual language as a result. While working on a charger design for Duracell, my design team visualized the powerful and dynamic brand message as a faceted surface to appeal to the target consumer. The facet officially and successfully unified Duracell products as a corporate guideline.

VDL can originate in an early phase of product development, which is practical to create preliminary design concepts. VDL mainly focuses on consumers and tries to figure out what they are demanding and their aspirations. Because the consumer market is changing all the time, VDL should be agile and responsive to social and market trends. When it comes to the lifestyle product categories, VDL should play a significant role, and identifying VDL is crucial to the success of the product.

2. VBL

VBL (Visual Brand Language) includes features of VDL, plus the holistic design approach that embraces the branding.

In addition to product design development, VBL provides a guideline for the packaging, the retail signage, and the brand visual applications. This guideline rules over the product line and helps the individual products to unify under the brand.

There is a plethora of consumer products out there. It is not surprising to see that engineers influence product design or other visual elements in favor of time and cost-savings. However, the consumers' experience of the products is related to their lifestyles, which is frequently transforming. Some product life cycles, such as smartphones, may be too short to ever catch up, but designers must find time to prepare for what comes next.

The highly competitive retail shelves often refer to a battlefield where major companies draw buyers' attention to their products. This effort directly relates to how the VBL is perceived through the products. It delivers brand messages from the company to consumers. VBL is visualizing the brand image that should be useful in advertising, packaging, social events, and so much more. The brand message is about benefits, reliability, satisfaction, and trust. Over time, consumers relate their product experience with the visual brand language. And the brand images become a foundation of consumer loyalty. VDL is often a complex task that deals with the core brand message the individual product delivers. After all, the most significant brand language should directly relate to what the consumers desire.

3. Unifier & Differentiator

Design elements can develop in a few different layers. Some layers are present in retail stores, and others can be found during use. These design elements can function in two different ways in VBL: Unifier and Differentiator.

Unifier is a common visual element that a series of products share to look related to one family. Design unifiers are powerful and bring significant value when many products show a single signature image for the many different product categories.

BMW's kidney grille is an excellent example with which each series of vehicles is tied together as one group. While the design unifier works throughout the product line, each product tactically needs to characterize the individual language that resonates with the precisely targeted consumer. Differentiating design elements are also essential when a company offers a broader product line for a wide range of consumers. BMW uses distinctive design language on each series of its vehicles to appeal to the targeted consumers. BMW 3 series demonstrates differentiated design with the curved and shallow body surfacing on theside profile, while the 7 series features the same part straighter and deep. It is an excellent example of how the unifier and differentiator can work together.

For another example, the Google Home Mini comes in four different color options. The colors function as great differentiators to reach younger consumers.

4. Signature Element

When design elements work for both unifier and differentiator well, we call it a Signature Element. The rule is that the signature element must be implemented consistently. It is how designers build brand equity and increase consumer recognition over time. The signature elements should be prominent and recognizable. These certified design elements often yield a brand image in the consumer-facing places such as retail stores or banners on the website. Well-located signature elements can miraculously draw potential customers' attention. They can find it from the crowded shelves in the mall or from a sponsored cameo-product[41] on TV shows.

BMW 303 used the earliest kidney grille as the brand's icon in the 1930s. This became a powerful signature element that visually ties up the many generations of the vehicle. This single signature element has contributed to consumers' perceived value and brand equity. (Figure 16)

---

[41] A cameo appearance is a brief appearance of a well-known person or product in a work of the performing arts, such as movies or TV shows.

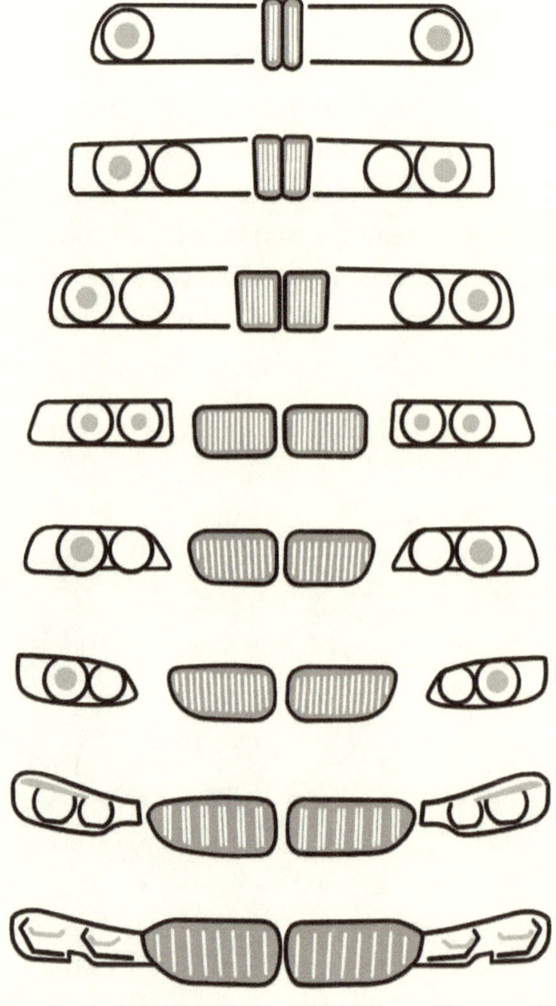

Figure 16 BMW 3 Series Kidney Grille (1966~2020)

The Dyson Cyclone [42] exemplifies a key signature element. The unique technology features a revolutionary technique that solves the everyday problem of vacuums' losing suction. The design team explicitly signified the cyclone tubing elements inside by specifying a transparent dust canister. It allows shoppers to see Cyclone tubes in the retail stores, and users can watch the uncompromising suction power inside. The famous signature element has been implemented consistently in the Original, Dual, and finally Multi Cyclone vacuum cleaners. It is an excellent example that an innovative feature can be a powerful signature element that could have been ignored otherwise.

5. Tiers

In retail business, it is common to separate low-end budget products from high-end premium ones. Not only do these products come with different functional benefits, but they discreetly personify the product's image according to the tiers in the market. These

---

[42] Revolutionary technology solved the everyday problem of vacuums losing suction invented by James Dyson in 1993.

images can help to position the products vertically to communicate the differentiated values and benefits in the product line. When designers define the premium market, the tiering strategy can be useful to visualize the products by utilizing relevant materials and quality finish, which can appeal to high-end consumers. Similarly, designers manipulate the design attributes for the lower tier product. They are more approachable with price-cautious materials, not only to reduce the cost, but to differentiate from the upper-tier product.

Product tiering can be best practiced with VBL (Visual Brand Language) to implement the whole product line, especially for the corporation.

6. Tactic

Many companies develop extraordinary design with a great strategy. On the flip side, the design is still a nice-to-have component for a small company (like startups). These organizations look for a tactical design approach that can serve for their limited budget and resource. These designs also can draw significant attention for renowned design awards competing with major corporations. Startups often focus on a tactical target consumer group and sculpt their product and service to meet the specific needs. As a good example, many startup companies team up with a great design agency to develop tactical designs and succeed in the early-stage market. For instance, VivaLnk[43] is an IoT-based startup that offers a wearable thermometer that measures temperature and sends it to smartphones. VivaLnk's patch-like multi-sensors vital tracking technology collaborated with a local design agency to develop a product that specifically targeted the medical category. The patch design successfully integrated with wireless sensors. A user-friendly application that streams real-time vitals data and the product packaging completed the overall product experiences. They named the device FeverScout, which is intended to be a skin-line wearable and iconic for the next generation of connected thermometers. The story of this product's development was widely shared in the community, and the product made a strong influence to merge between consumer electronics and medical devices.

---

[43] ioT based Medical equipment supplier in Campbell, California

09 _SERVICE

Companies like Procter & Gamble contend that marketers have the best chance of converting a browser into a buyer by appealing to their senses, values, and emotions.[44] When consumers see a brand-new product in the retail store or on-line environment, the product is most likely surrounded by competitors in an overwhelming marketplace.

In the highly competitive retail environment, the very first moment of showcasing the product to a protentional consumer is significantly important. The moment opens up the new opportunity of the market. That is why many companies work specifically hard to grasp the moment to appeal to consumers. If the product successfully communicates in the retail environments, the chances are high for products to survive and succeed

---

[44] Actionable Marketing Guide, coined by Procter & Gamble

in the market. However, this is only the time of making purchasing decisions, and the most critical product experience follows after that.

First Moment of Truth

As the design team effort delivers the product into the retail environment where all the competitors are gathering, it only takes a few seconds for shoppers to turn themselves into buyers. The marketing team names the prime time 'First Moment of Truth' (FMOT), and they have measured the moment as only 3-7 seconds long. [45] Consumers are consolidating useful information and trying to convince themselves of a purchase as intellectually as possible. Some of them will come up with a buying decision meticulously, while others just do it instantly. However, they still count on their rationale and experience to be a proud consumer. Then, how can designers help design to communicate the best with potential buyers in the crucial moments? How can design maximize the chance to convince the consumers' behavior in a blink of a second?

For full design support during the FMOT, the team can find a way to provide a design story or a

---

[45] The First Moment of Truth (FMOT, pronounced EFF-mot), is the 3-7 seconds after a shopper first encounters a product on a store shelf

testimonial that proves the story. Social media engagement will play an essential role in this phase. There are a handful of design awards that are active for business promotion. After all, customers are close to purchasing at this time, so they are seeking answers to specific questions. Designers can find a way to predict possible queries and should be able to provide prompt responses. The answers can lay on the package, the signage, or social media. There are four ways designers should consider during the FMOT. It is relatively lower hanging fruits that they should not miss. Because, if the design team does not supply solutions, others in shoppers' networks, including your competitors, will.

1. Art of Review

There's always a discrepancy between what is intended and what is perceived in design. Minimizing the gap can be the key to success in design communication. A design language can be found in many different ways. One may love it, while others hate the same thing. It is a subject matter whether it is received the way intended or not. However, designers can help better control how to deliver the visual message to the consumers in a way intended. The art of visual communication of designing for FMOT takes multiple steps to get it through. There are always diverse opinions from different perspectives during the design process. However, when they are getting closer to the objective viewpoint, the common denominator appears and grows.

One well-qualified technique to verify design communication in the retail environment is using marketing team reviews. Through the multiple team reviews, designers can enhance the quality of communication, so that the work reflects the design intents as articulated. A thorough review always takes a significant focus on primary concepts and design intents to communicate for consumers. Communication is often challenging and gives designers a hurdle to get over. But the focused reviews can build a strong and confident visual solution that is likely to convince consumers in the same way designers had to do to the reviewers.

2. Corporate Identity

While a product design has the intrinsic values to show through its appearances, Corporate Identity uses the consistent visual assets representing the company. The visual images usually characterize the brand and consumers. A proper corporate identity depicts the organization's core message so that shoppers can easily recognize and remember. The consistent and well-identified corporate image will identify the senses, values, and emotions of their consumers. It can most effectively work at diverse locations and retail environments by using a single visual language to deliver corporate identity.

3. Vibe

We are facing countless numbers of human-made commodities every day. Consumers have the privilege of choice of many products and services. As the choice of products reflects their need, value, and characteristic, products lay in the retail space accordingly. Because some design languages fit their home, while others do not, consumers bring a significant consideration to make a curated image of product choice to represent who they are. The curated image identifies the Vibe.

Consumers are immediately drawn and triggered by products and services, resonating with a specific vibe that they like. As I mentioned in 01_CONSUMER Experience, a lifestyle-reflecting image can be found in a second when they are shopping for products and services. Some consumers are interested in collecting their vibe, referred from television shows and magazines, and often obtain those images on Pinterest boards. In fashion, a brochure categorizes personal preferences that clusters by market trends. One style comes in while others go out. The periodic style transition, as it is called a design trend, should be watched. There are many trends to be considered in color, finish, and material selection, as well as the form. The trendy vibes, like other vital features, are crucial players to influence consumers in the first moment of truth.

4. Banner

We follow arrows for direction. Many signs are universally communicating everyday life. Those signs use a visual image to depicts useful information. In retail banners or physical stores, the signage effectively supports delivering the product's core message and functional benefits.

The signage is efficient, even though it is relatively easy to build as it is a temporary element supporting the actual product. The product's primary feature on the banner should easily communicate. The banner design can simply follow the visual design language if available. However, banner can directly resonate with the consumers' vibe as it intends to draw their attention in the first moment of truth.

Brand Equity

The great brand that consumers associate with excellent products and services delivers essential messages. A brand, representing a corporation, is what consumers see and remember for products and services offered. The brand's visual logo and embedded message have the power to visualize the quality service. The design and marketing team should make sure that the brand messages relate to the consumers and the society where they live. It is always essential that a great product leverages the positive brand image that consumers already associate with. Brand Equity is an intangible corporate property that designers should be aware of. The quality product supports the brand equity, and brand equity helps the quality product succeed in return.

1. Brand Perception

Brand equity, by definition, is referring to the perceived worth of a brand in and of itself. The social value of a well-reputed brand can give credit to a new product when released in the market, while the same product with an unrecognized brand may have a longer time to convince the same consumers. Thus, the social value of a great brand is sometimes worth more than the products they sell.[46] The company of a well-perceived brand can grow faster directly from brand perception. As you can imagine, brand equity can't build overnight but takes significant time and

---

[46] Managing Brand Equity by David A. Aaker

dedication through quality products and services.

Every consumer has their favorite brand in their mind. When consumers trust a brand, they stay with that product. The best part is that consumers like to share extraordinary brand experiences with friends and family, furthermore, to the community. It is one of the reasons that a great product with a well-perceived brand grows fast.
Trusted brands are associated with all product categories, such as cars, smartphones, fashion, retail, institutions, and of course, food. The trusted brand typically sets up its brand story proactively on their website. Yeti, the outdoor gear company, is an excellent example of a successful brand story that is perceived to the outdoor enthusiasts.

An example of how brand perception leveraged design development can be found with Friedrich, an air-conditioning company with a century-long legacy. People have been living with the convenience of what their products offer. As the company grows, customers are aging, and they recall how the product had served on hot summer days. In Los Angeles and New York City, researchers and designers talked to people who used the

Friedrich air-conditioner and asked what comes to mind when looking at Friedrich as a brand. They said things like, 'American-made-commercial-grade.' As the phrase depicts, the interviewees recalled that the product was robust and durable with the excellent build quality. The research debriefs helped the design team ideate specifically how to resonate with the brand message. As a typical approach to explore the sketch brainstorm, the team developed sketch concepts to leverage what Friedrich's customers remember.

After a couple of sketch sessions, our design team created robust and timeless design languages. The concept also reflected the contemporary image that should ideally blend in urban apartments, since the units would be wall-mounted. Best of all, the concept story precisely handed over the brand heritage that the clients and the team made a confident decision to move forward with the product development. The work had successfully resonated with the client's invaluable brand perception. All product lines are now sharing the same design language as its predecessor had established for the brand.

2. Brand Image

A group effort can elevate the brand image. The job designers do every day may not have a direct impact on it, but it does have an incremental influence. Technically, a visual brand image relies on the marketing or design team. But the effort should be collaborative teamwork to improve and steer in the right direction.

The direction of a brand image should, in marketing, reflect a message that the brand promises to the customers at present and the future. While the marketing articulates plans, the actual product is created and manipulated by hands-on designers and developers. It is always challenging to synchronize those teams to make harmonized results. Designers and engineers can make a great product, but the product image may target irrelevant consumers. As a result, a brand image can mistakenly deliver. A brand image of excellent product design can be so powerful that it can exceed the consumer's expectation and accelerate the company's effort to succeed. As I mentioned in 8_VALUE Design Language, this is one of the reasons the brand image as a strategic marketing component needs to align with the VBL (Visual Brand Language) that projects the brand.

3. Product Name

A product name can be descriptive of how the product will work for the users. As the development team chooses a product name, it grants an opportunity that the title will always present in the prime location of the product.

As the team explores the product design concepts and creates inspiration boards, designers come up with multiple design concept names. Those names entitle individual ideas. These exercises can yield consumer-facing product name candidates. Although the product names are usually different from the internal concept name, the name can explain the core benefits that the product will deliver for the users. Furthermore, a product name can apply as a series of product lines that represent consumer categories and price tiers.

For example, iMac is a great name of the Internet and Macintosh, representing the revolutionary browsing application and Apple's original Macintosh. Ken Segall, an employee of the LA advertising agency, says that the 'i' stands for 'internet' but also represents the product as a personal and revolutionary device ('i' for individuality and innovation).[47] Mac was short for Macintosh, which was a core business that stands for the brand. Consequently, two words were married into iMac, which is the simple name that works a tremendous job for the company. Apple later adopted the 'i' prefix across its consumer hardware and software lines, such as iCalendar, iBook, and other applications such as the iLife, iWork, and iTunes[48].

---

[47] "The First iMac Introduction". YouTube. January 30, 2006. Retrieved July 6, 2011.

[48] Media player, media library, Internet radio broadcaster and mobile device management utility for iTunes Store, developed by Apple

10_DELIVER

Storytelling

An idea remains only an idea until it is told to others. Storytelling can magically transform a rough idea into an actionable product concept. Thus, designers can utilize story-telling to help primitive ideas grow. Storytelling can be useful throughout the development process. Because the ritual part of telling a story forces a designer to empathize with the intrinsic value of the core ideas, storytelling is a significant part of design development. Telling the stories of our routines is so essential, like the water we drink, but we often neglect the importance of it. Storytelling is a powerful tool. As we narrate a story with what we observe, it brings meaning to our lives. Through telling a story, we discover important issues and opportunities in our daily experiences.

Design language can be truly empowered when it tells us a user story. Developing the story takes a process from acknowledging the background where problems originate and the unmet needs to the profitable solution. The intriguing story often comes from understanding what users are suffering from. Unlike advertising, which highlights products' functional aspects, design stories can personify the consumer and their characteristics. During the concept development, multiple product concepts are reviewed, and each concept can represent a related 'concept story' to characterize the consumers.

1. Concept Story

Designers develop concepts. Usually, a design concept development is about looking for functional benefits that elevate the product experience. Finding a good design concept demands observation and listening to the problem to offer better experiences. Concept storytelling starts from here. The concept story development requires a closer look at how a user would perceive the product in their mind. Designers classify users on categories and personify who they are. These activities may combine with consumer analysis, from the marketing team, which categorizes strategic consumer groups.

An excellent concept story requires manifesting design attributes, which can be an excellent source for designers to ideate. A design inspiration-board is one example that visualizes the concept story. The complete concept story can show the image of consumers and their lifestyle and iterate the design attributes that characterize the consumers. An excellent concept story should be self-explanatory, but designers can tell the story to the internal team or potential consumers to prove it.

2. Concept Family Story

An individual product has its own story to tell. Furthermore, a product can become a member of a product group. The series of products can exist for different reasons, such as regional and seasonal differences. Product design can tell differentiated benefits while they intend to look unified. We call it 'Concept Family Story.' The concept family story development can be a comprehensive exercise to define the corporate design language, which is significantly essential for an organization that offers a series of products and services. (Figure 17)

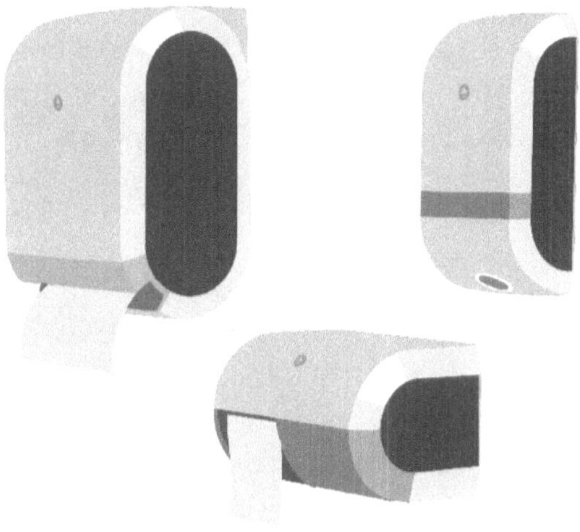

Figure 17 GP Pro Concept Family Story

Sketch

Sketching is an excellent tool for storytelling. While 'language arts' uses words to depict a story, the great design utilizes sketches to tell the concept story. The sketch is the oldest visual form of human expression of ideas. A drawing can illustrate unlimited functional and emotional characteristics. The hand sketch is like a human choreography, expressing dynamic and calm or joyful and heavy feelings with visual gesture and its movement. The sketch is not limited to artists or designers, but anyone can use the fascinating tool to express themselves. The hard part of utilizing the ancient skill is that it takes training to master it. But the tradeoff is the more you train yourself, the better hand-drawn expression belongs to you.

1. Sketch vs. CAD

Not long ago, when there was no computer-aided visualization available, the sketch form was the most preferred method to demonstrate design concepts. With the help of CAD (computer-aided design), design visualization has taken advantage of the technology. But can CAD replace hand-sketches? The short answer is 'no.' There is a simple reason why sketch should not be an optional tool, especially for designers.

There are two completely different types of design demonstration. The first one is the concept development visualization, and the other is the concept refinement visualization. For the former visualization, designers need the skill to populate multiple idea expressions in a short time, while the latter presentation can rely on computer-aided design. If designers use computers in an early phase, it may take a long time, and the designer's creativity will be limited. If they use the hand-drawn sketch for the final concept visualization, it will be hard to show the engineering details and accuracy. As a result, combining sketch and CAD will be the most productive tools the design team can always use.

2. Sketchbook

Like a poet takes quick notes on their journal when they have ideas, a designer should be nimble to capture design inspiration in his or her sketchbook. When the sketches accumulate as a whole idea, it can be a potential seed for early concept development. In addition to personal use, a sketch form can be instrumental in demonstrating the nuance of form details. A simple line can visualize from the minimal gesture to the complex movement. A simple form can express from the still pose to the dynamic gesture. An array of differentiated sketches can facilitate a productive conversation, and it can strategically help the design team to choose the best aesthetics. The best part of using a sketch is that it can populate countless ideas on the wall and be a practical tool to help the design team to consolidate the leading concepts.

3. Power Sketch

Power sketches can speak much more. They can visualize aesthetic proportions that are directly related to mechanical configurations. Because simple sketch forms can better communicate the core ideas, it can quickly compare the opposing concepts to make a team decision.

A great sketch is influential to the internal audience, just like art is appealing to people. Sketches for consumer goods can reflect either a dynamic or minimal lifestyle by differentiating sketch line contrast and weight. A great sketch can also reflect the designer's personality. Some designers' sketches can be festive and expressive, while others are sophisticated and precise. However, regardless of designers' characteristics, the sketch form should be a universal tool to visualize ideas and quickly allow the team to make a prompt decision to move forward.

4. Sketch board

Developing a great sketch varies depending on what you need because some sketch requires a skill of the technical perspective in three-dimensional space. In contrast, other sketches only need to illustrate rough ideas in a simple two-dimensional line drawing. As I mentioned on 03_EGO TO ECO Design Social, the Pinterest board can be a great place to learn numerous sketch forms professional designers have already developed. Through the sketch reference board, anyone should be able to train themselves to develop a great sketch. For a professional sketch training at school, students can learn from the basic pencil sketch to the computer-aided rendering. Designers often focus on CAD and neglect the chance to improve productive hand sketches. However, it is crucial to keep both visualizations balanced to get the best results.

Just as words are the primary element of language arts, a sketch is essential for significant design development. When designers use more sketch forms as a productive storytelling tool, they can better focus on the core problem while not being distracted by secondary details. Through the sketches, all the ideas drawn can be conveniently archived to be accessed for future reference.

Creative Fuel

Is creativity a personal trait which one is naturally born with? Or is it a skill to learn? Everyone has different opinions on this, however here is a great saying,

"Openness to experience… is the single strongest and most consistent personality trait that predicts creative achievement," [49]
-James C. Kaufman

Creativity is a mindset that is undefined, completely open, and always ready to change. With this mindset, anyone can be creative, regardless. Thus, open-mindedness can be as important as creativity. Creative energy is a driving force that fuels creative ideas. Designers use inspiration and motivation to boost their creative energy.

Creative people change the world, but they rarely command it. The eighteenth-century industrial revolution won the credit of the most innovative

---

[49] Creativity 101, James C. Kaufman is an American psychologist known for his research on creativity.

design development, but the settlers gained the title of business success. Designers inspire corporate success, but then the leadership often settles down until they see another challenge or even destroy what they already developed. "Creative people are in the process of winning and are positioned to achieve professional success, a more vibrant creative culture, and a happier world."[50] As Esslinger wrote, the creative energy and its application to the community is taking place.

1. Inspiration

When Jony Ive and his design team had secretly been working on the first iPhone, there was one image on their mind, 'The infinity pool.'[51]

A perfectly clean and uninterrupted edge showcases an infinite surface of water that works as a natural mirror for the sky while minimizing visual noise around it. Just like the infinity pool was an idea starter for a successful product, great inspiration can do a significant job for designers.

Inspiration works as an ultimate catalyzer for a creative process. Everyone has sources of

---

[50] Hartmut Esslinger, DesignForward, Creative strategies for sustainable change

[51] Joney Ive: The genius behind Apple's greatest product

inspiration. To find these external catalyzers, teams use travel, movies, and reading, which is abundant with fruitful sources.

A great mentor can be an internal accelerator, influential and resulting in significant impact on the quality of products. [52] In an early development phase, plenty of inspiration can come from connecting people with different perspectives. When we are willing to connect to people whom we like to understand, this can naturally reveal an entirely new view, and thus can yield the greatest inspiration. Therefore, interpersonal skills can deliver significant sources for team inspiration. "A person's success in life can usually be measured by the number of uncomfortable conversations he or she is willing to have with others," said Tim Ferriss[53].

Great inspiration can be fostered and shared in the same interest group through social media. Thus, product development and design activities are encouraged to leverage the social network as an inspirational source. What we are looking for is mostly out there.

---

[52] The laws of Simplicity by John Maeta
[53] Timothy Ferriss: an American entrepreneur, author, and podcaster.

It is just a matter of how to find and make the inspiration useful.

2. Motivation

Motivation starts with people. It always springs out from oneself and branches outward to influence others. High motivation is always rooted in experiences, whether it is suffering or ecstatic moments. When you love doing something, that will likely yield a positive consequence. But when you feel no interest in doing the same task, you will probably not conclude the same result.

As a part of human nature, motivation can grow in a community where the same interest group meets together and looks for a common goal. In the creative industries, motivation is a crucial fuel to run creative activities. High motivation is contagious and yields team morale.

Motivation can be cross-pollinating. Great motivation can be followed and used to inspire the development team to implement it in the real world. For example, Dieter Ram is an excellent motivator for many designers and documented in his '10 Principles of Good Design' and its execution on the actual products, such as a legendary transistor Radio T3 (1958). James Dyson is another insightful design-engineer acknowledged for the 'Tenacious Innovation' of the Cyclone technology and its visual presentation as a signature element.

Frank Lloyd Wright's 'Fallingwater' has been referred to as the minimalistic and geometric aesthetic that is prevailing today. Issey Miyake's 'the spontaneous origami' structures motivated the futuristic BAO BAO bag design (Figure 18).

Figure 18 Issey Miyake Collapsible Tote Bag

Harry Bertoia, a renowned sculptor of his time, created 'Streamlined Structural Art' that influenced the legendary diamond chair (Figure 19), which is still selling with a high price tag since 1953. Susan Kara is one of the greatest graphic designers, pioneering thousands of icons on digital space for leading companies around the world.

Figure 19 Harry Bertoia Outdoor Chair

3. Emotion

How would you build an emotional connection between the user and the product? Emotion is a unique creative fuel that is hard to see, and in turn, hard to verify.

Investment in the emotional aspects of a product may not relate to a direct return. However, emotional design engraves a mark on consumers' minds. Just like form follows function, users follow emotion. The more emotional elements in a product, the better it will be. Because the humanizing elements can relate care, affection, love, and warm behavior, the emotional design can enhance ROE (Return on Emotion) as a result.

4. Passion

Passion comes from individuals. A passionate designer can bring positive energy that the team can share. In product development, passion should be valued and taken care of to generate creative ingredients and innovative ideas. Passion is like 'the high octane super-premium fuel.' It runs the creative engine to high performance.

For product development, some designers may work on passion, while others do the same job for compensation. Unlike a routine task, the design development uses unique dynamics depending on who are the team members and how they approach the task. There are many layers of quality design and execution. Excellent product development is always awarded by the consumers and proudly exposed to the community. Those products likely stand for the passionate team.

Passion, an extraordinary force, makes the team go beyond what is expected—aiming for what they desire on behalf of their consumers. A great brand is not likely planned, but instead occurs as a result of a passionate team.

| REMEMBER & USE |

Focusing on purpose will help to make a design rationale for the team to utilize and ensure greater success for the product and service development.

Focusing on users' pain points and identifying the core problems is extremely important.
The development team can utilize the creative force to unveil problems and provide quality solutions.

Focusing on human attributes, such as intellectual aspects of who the consumers are, will help to focus on the market opportunity. One humanizing interaction that designers can learn from is how consumers 'play' with a product.

Design value is tangible when it is consistently applicable to the product and service. Setting up the design language will guide the team to empathize with the design value and will be an excellent tool for an organizational guideline.

Understanding retail is as essential as developing products. Focusing on the FMOT will identify the essential part of product benefits that should be prioritized. Brand perception began from a retail environment and complete with product experience to build brand equity.

Storytelling is an excellent way of developing product ideas. The team can use quick sketches to visualize initial ideas and verify whether the thoughts are viable or unfeasible. The team can use the design fuel to excel in the concept delivery.

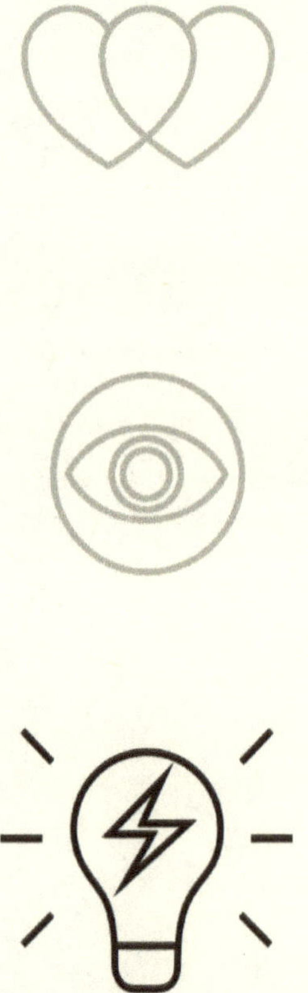

| PART 3 |

DISRUPT MINDSET

As designers, we have to see beyond existing technology and ask, 'Is there a better way?' [54]

-James Dyson

---

[54] Inventor, industrial designer, and entrepreneur who founded Dyson Ltd.

Part 3: DISRUPT

11_ PROCESS
Innovation
Design Virtue

12_ MARKET
Competition

13_ BUSINESS
Startup
Intellectual Property
Reward

11_PROCESS

"The world that we have created is the result of an obsolete mindset. The problems that have resulted cannot be solved with the same mindset that caused that."[55]
-Albert Einstein

Every designer and engineer are talking about innovation. Innovation is one common goal to achieve, and the great result out of it is rewarding. Innovation is, by definition, the action or process of making changes in something established, especially by introducing new methods, ideas, or products. There are two things to discuss regarding innovation. Why do we innovate and how?

---

[55] Albert Einstein, German-born theoretical physicist

Innovation

As Design Recipe addresses, design is a construction of an object or the implementation of an activity. As the industry grows and technology becomes standardized, designers look for new ways to improve products and services. Excellent design innovation can improve production and consumer experiences. Innovative ideas can improve products' integrity, reduce cost in manufacturing and distribution, and ultimately enhance the product experience for users.

The Unibody design for the MacBook [56] is an excellent example of design innovation. The machined aluminum body was a surprisingly innovative idea the design team initiated and developed. There was a list of 60 reasons from the manufacturer why the unibody won't work. [57] The most innovative notebook computer housing has delivered the thinnest computer profile that can fit into the brown clasp envelope. In addition to that, it provided the highest construction integrity compared to competitors.

---

[56] MacBook is Macintosh portable computer series developed and sold by Apple Inc.
[57] Jony Ive, The Genius Behind Apple's Greatest Products by Leander Kahney

MacBook's design challenge was visual simplicity that grants the most significant user experience that can be perceived as well as seen. The unibody minimized a visible parting line outside and the number of construction parts inside, which eventually simplified the manufacturing procedure. They also get credit for using highly recyclable material, which could not be possible in traditional plastic construction. Design work is evolving from building an attractive product to a comprehensive activity where innovation works at the core. With consistent design innovation, the product development team can truly cross-pollinate and succeed.

1. Innovation Basic

Real innovation is possible when the team understands the complete layers of a product: the more knowledgeable they are of a product and its purpose, the higher chance the team can innovate in the product experience. Even if innovation brings value and consumers' benefits, it takes cost and time. Typically, successful innovation accompanies the cost analysis and close collaboration with manufacturers. Without that, innovative ideas are likely dropped and forgotten. Thus, innovation should be contemplated with crucial data to convince the internal team and manufacturer. Great innovation motivates and educates internal teams, and enhances the consumer experience as a result. When the design team has convincing data and collaborates with extended engineering teams, successful innovation will be an achievable goal.

2. Concurrent Engineering

Innovative products frequently derive from an intimate collaboration between engineers and designers. These two groups work closely from the idea exploration to the refinement phases. They often work as one team in a shared studio space. We call it Concurrent Engineering.

Contour [58] was a startup company that commissioned Ziba Design[59] to develop an action sports camera for extreme enthusiasts. The camera included multiple design challenges such as robust unit architecture, a reliable and flexible mounting system,

---

[58] POV action sport camera venture / startup
[59] Design consultancy located in Portland, Oregon

picture calibration, and intuitive shooting and sharing interface.

Ziba set up a special team and assigned a designated war room and resource of several engineers and designers to innovate on the camera. Concurrent engineering took an unprecedentedly short time to articulate all of the challenges and develop a completely new camera with a strong design language. The team built crude prototypes to verify unit-integrity, ergonomics, mounting mechanism, usability, and content shooting and sharing. The result was a robust and durable camera design that integrates with the multi-directional sliding mount system, laser calibration, and shock-proof unit construction. As the design came out in the market, the product was immediately adopted by the extreme sports community, and the content was quickly captured and shared. Several design awards also buoyed the success of the camera. (Figure 17)

Figure 20 Contour Helmet Mount Camera

3. Mindset

Innovation only comes from an innovative mindset. Great innovation yields a unique and relevant product to meet a precisely targeted consumer. A creative mindset amongst team members is contagious and naturally develops team morale, which is an invaluable asset for the organization. Best of all, innovative product results in immediate brand awareness in the market and makes the business viable.

Design Virtue

"Wisdom is knowing what to do next, skill is knowing how to do it, and virtue is doing it."[60]

Let's say that one team member says, "Hey, that is my idea," and the other follows, "I thought about that." We have to admit that initiating a great idea should be credited, but bringing the concept to the real world should be rewarded because it takes a significant commitment and dedication. Only a small fraction of great ideas has an opportunity to develop and launch in the market. During the product development process, it takes many decisions and responsibilities. Doing so, the team grows solid and learns the way to survive and to succeed in the market. There are multiple steps in product development, and nothing is more critical than executing the idea into the real world.

---

[60] David Starr Jordan, Educator, former president of Stanford University,

1. Brainstorming

There is no crazy idea in the brainstorm because insane ideas evolve into great ones. Many innovative thoughts originated from brainstorming. How does brainstorming work? Every brainstorm is different, and each one has its organizer who intends to achieve a goal. There are a handful of techniques to maximize the result.

A brainstorm organizer can hand-select the participants who best fit the task to achieve. The organizer can invite participants in person one at a time, brief the topic, and even give them the assignment to start their involvement earlier. The goal should be presented at the beginning so the team can focus on the targeted task. It should be clear that each member participates so that the brainstorm can generate a certain number of ideas at the end. A great idea is often derived from a large group of ideas. The organizer should free their mind so the team can be creative. Google's co-founder said, "Good ideas are always crazy until they're not." [61]

---

[61] Larry Page, cofounder of Google

A limited time won't limit the idea. The time limit encourages participants to generate ideas within a set amount of time and make the brainstorm dynamic. The organizer can inform the time-limit for participants to accelerate the dynamic. Ideas grow as members share during the brainstorm. Listening to others' ideas and building on them is always a productive and efficient way of brainstorming. It is great fun to watch how ideas evolve.

2. Prototype

Designers do not *generate* ideas on a computer. They only *implement* ideas on a computer. The design manifestation is only possible through appropriate visualization and a prototype that proliferates and improvises potent ideas. Designers are encouraged to allow accidents by prototyping ideas. Having a designated space where the accidents can happen, such as a model-making room, helps designers to explore prototypes. Interestingly, many great designs and solutions occur by accident in the model shop.

During prototyping, integrating and relating elements together, such as forms and details, may not work, so designers are encouraged to disintegrate and re-associate them until they work. It can develop several configurations for the team to review, and the exercise is a great way to come up with an optimal solution. A rule that designers should avoid is something in between, neither associated nor disassociated. Distinctive features that are forced to blend into one form can lose the honesty, and adding fake (unnecessary) visual elements can lose the simplicity.

It is useful to look at design in both three-dimensional (sculptural) and two dimensional (graphical) aspects. Designers are encouraged to alternate between these two aspects as they work. They can relate the two-dimensional design into the three-dimensional form, which surprisingly works well. A successful design should orchestrate with the user, the environment, the brand, and the project brief, which gives all the clues of form and details.

3. Keep It Simple

Keeping the product simple is not as simple as it sounds. There is always a list of reasons that make the product complex. But why is simple design better? Because simplicity helps to concentrate on the essential aspects, and the product is not burdened with non-essentials. [62]One way of achieving a simple design is hiding the purposeful features so that users can find the essential parts intuitively during the product experience. If every functional feature stands out equally, it can confuse and mislead users.

There is another reason to keep the product simple. Through the process of the product experience, simple design approaches the users intuitively, and they can enjoy the product service beyond functionality. As I mentioned 5_PURPOSE Rationale, the emotional design requires focusing on nothing but an essential part of the product. When products exist to show everything, it will get complicated pretty quickly, and the user will have a hard time finding the product enjoyable.

---

[62] Dieter Rams, 10 principles for good design

4. Checkpoint

Every designer has their motivation to drive the project. They are sometimes making progress and other times stuck with issues with unexpected problems. The good thing is that the team grows through the process. Growing as a professional designer requires confrontation of many hurdles, dealing with people, budget, and deadline.

Through the lengthy and tiring process, a team leader can suggest setting the Checkpoint where each stage of effort can be reviewed and qualified to move to the next step. Each milestone will mark as a base camp where the future direction can branch out, so even other teams can work towards the goal, making sure that a set of previous work is still valid to refer to when needed. Using a checkpoint is a great way to utilize time efficiently without wasting resources.

5. Deadline

Ironically, good design is to exercise within constraints. Many designers are working with limited resources and an aggressive deadline. When they deal with the circumstances, ideas are not limited, but instead, designers can focus more on the essence of the issues to resolve. "When you work with resources that are restricted in what you can do with them, the designer focuses on the real problems and issues." [63]

---

[63] Charles and Ray Eames, Industrial Designers who made significant contribution to the development of modern architecture and furniture

12_MARKET

"Design should be holistic and grow from both inside and outside. If applied only on the outside, it can easily be rubbed off by the first contact with the competition." [64]

Competition

We are living in a society where industrial technology is standardized and approachable. The price of personal computers has been cut in half in recent years, while the performance doubled soon after another. Massive OLED screen TVs are now more affordable for everyone, while the image quality offered is unprecedented.

During our time of fast-moving technology, where in the market is the real competition remaining? How

---

[64] Sohrab Vossoughi, founder of Ziba Design, a design and innovation consultancy based in Portland, OR

can designers manipulate their activities that should lead to a highly competitive market place? What do they need to do to keep their design unique and relevant in the market? To answer these questions, the design team must look at the market either directly or indirectly, analyze the market trends, and locate the opportunity space of their business.

1. Secondary Research

It is hard to start design development from scratch. It should preferably be initiated from reliable data that motivates a specific design direction. Whether the project has a budget to utilize time and resources, designers should find a way to search for relevant information and data with which to begin the project.

Secondary research is free and takes a relatively short time to do, but the results are productive. Secondary research can be done by web searching, reading magazines, or simply watching the market. Having the useful resources at hand is extremely important to understand competitors and products in the market. Looking at the competitive landscape will help the design team move away from a saturated market and will help the team to ideate a unique and distinctive design concept direction.

2. Competitive Analysis

When it comes to consumer products and services, the markets are highly saturated, and consumers may already have a wide range of product choices. Looking at the market competition is a crucial step for designers, and the activity will direct the product design to be competent in the market.

A 'competitive analysis map' can visually position competitors' products and show market trends. The map can help to identify a space where specific design languages are saturated and how high the competition is in a particular market. The map also changes over time. The transition on the map can reveal a flow of market trends, and thus provide a forecast of the new design direction. Where the market is heading can provide useful insights from which the product can associate to lead its way in the competitive market.

3. Opportunity Space

As always, market opportunities are unlimited. However, a real opportunity should motivate the team so that the development proceeds until the final product is delivered to consumers. In reality, the chances are immediately narrowed down if the opportunities have to be viable and profitable in business. But, how can the design team bring the design activities to fruition? It is a valid question that the team must continue to answer until they finalize the job.

Hypothetically, the design concepts and their ability to appeal to consumers can be foreseen and manipulated. To do that, the design team needs reliable data from field research or secondary research.
The research is beneficial for designers to support and validate the design concept. When designers can identify a market opportunity, design can develop accordingly. As a result, the product stands strong amongst competitors.

4. Design Positioning

In a 'competitive analysis map,' there is a position where the design team targets the design language. The Design Position will define the product and brand image in the market. The visual position should resonate with what the brand message is about and how the product and service are perceived.

Design positioning is also a great tool to differentiate product design. Without the differentiation, a design may helplessly blend into the highly competitive market without appealing to the target consumers.
The competitive landscape will point to an untouched market where the design opportunity resides and help teams stay away from the competition.

Successful products should be comprehensive. Through the development process, the product concept should grow from the outside, where unique design language is valid in the market. At the same time, it should develop from the inside where innovative and creative design can be of support. If a product grows holistically from both inside and outside, it will stand firm in the highly competitive market and will deliver unique benefits and services.

13_BUSINESS

Startup

Design activities, as a typical sequence, usually follow mechanical and electronic engineering developments. But this process is not helpful for innovation. As I explained on 11_PROCESS Innovation, an innovative design requires collaborating with the engineering and marketing team to come up with a genuinely innovative concept to win in the market.

When a no brand startup wanted a mobile security device that can be activated when a user confronts a life-threatening situation, Ziba was commissioned to develop the tiny lifesaver in an aggressive schedule. The engineering and design team collaboratively initiated the brainstorming to design and verify the engineering to meet the deadline. The target consumers were quickly defined, and several configurational prototypes were printed for the team to review. The concurrent engineering would not be possible unless it was planned ahead of time as a team decision. Sharing a single space for the whole team to work together was crucial to make the collaborative approach successful.

The 2020 CES (consumer electronics show) hosted more than 1,200 startups to 'Eureka Park,' the birthplace of future technologies. The startups focus on new business categories that are significant in the market in the future. The industries are often releasing cutting-edge technology and its first-time implementation to the market. What follows are some industry categories that many startups are focused on, such as IoT and healthcare related products. It was interesting to see where they are heading and who will lead the way to the future.

1. Autonomous

We have been witnessing the most exciting time where modern technology is infused with machine-learning algorithms to create products and services that have never existed before.

Camera sensors capture the live flow of commuters to coordinate how frequently they should run the public transportation service in major cities. Lidar on the lawn-care robot autonomously scans the height of the grass to cut the grass on time for the home owner's peace of mind.

Stanford Vision-lab is working on image scanning, dealing with 15 million digital photos. With the extensive image data, the lab is developing an intelligent algorithm to translate visual images into literal sentences. The self-learning computer is smart enough to identify a particular, incidental moment so that it can serve to prevent children from a life-threatening situation. As Dr. Fei Fei Li said on TED talk, image scanning and artificial intelligence technology are taking baby steps today and will influence many industries soon. [65]

2. IoT (Internet of Things)

Consumers are willing to pay for their piece of mind. IoT technology mostly interconnects with 'the smart home,' including home security systems and other home appliances such as thermostats,

---

[65] "How we teach computers to understand pictures, Stanford University, Vision and Learning Lab

security cameras, and many others. The IoT devices individually connect into ecosystems that control via smartphones and smart speakers.

IoT is a promising concept for consumables and their distribution. The scattered technologies are continually looking at customers' routine transactions and automatically reorder products and services. Amazon is affiliating with manufacturers to develop a smart package solution that is connected with the service providers to auto-replenish when the product contents run out. The auto-replenishment technology will not only satisfy consumers but collect prompt consumer behavior data for the company to serve the real-time market needs.

3. Life Science

The 2020 CES held in Las Vegas featured numerous medical instruments that appear as friendly consumer electronics. They are categorized as Life Science products. They introduced the ECG (electrocardiogram), sleep monitor, glucose monitors, and other healthcare products. In 2020, startups brought hearing aids, vision aids, robotic prosthetics, and much more.[66]

It is exciting to see the life science category meets specific medical needs, and proudly introduce an industry that bridges between medical-care and life-enhancing products. Digital health, connected medical systems, and health information and intelligence are rapidly growing, and the industry opens up new business opportunities.

The ECG monitors the heart rate and wires vital data to the healthcare provider. Not long ago, this could have only been serviced by ECG medical equipment in the hospital. Putting ECG sensors on the body could mean the patient is under a stigmatic impression that requires institutional service. Recently, wearable ECG functions not only for medical care but for wellness, which informs the best heart performance for fitness. The traditional ECG equipment design features safe and clean images such as white colors with a lot of stereotypical medical elements. Today, modern ECG wearable devices resonate with dynamic lifestyles or friendly consumer product images.

---

[66] The 2019 Consumer Electronics Show, Las Vegas

Designers can intentionally bring approachable visual elements instead of stigmatic medical images. As a result, what we had perceived as the pharmaceutical space will gradually turn into the all-new space where healthier and enhanced well-being can be reassured and will offer peace of mind for the consumers.

Food is another growing industry for startups. An autoimmune protocol diet is a new food-based diet approach to eliminate unwanted inflammation in a person's body. It's a diet that's thought to help heal our gut to reduce inflammation created by autoimmune conditions and requires us to avoid highly processed food. The food industry will share insights based on life science and will likely change the way consumers eat every day. For example, the diet-sensor device uses spectrometry for chemical analysis to check a user's meal calories and nutrition information is stored in the cloud. When found, it then sends the info to your phone via Bluetooth and creates a food log for the users to monitor and manage their diet. As life science grows into a practical application by startups, it will change the traditional health and wellness market and will positively lead consumer behavior.

4. AIP

AIP (Aging in Place) is one of the fastest-growing industries as the Boomers turn into seniors who have financial capability. The AIP movement for seniors is quite different from previous generations, who simply looked for retirement communities and secured lives. Even though Baby Boomers may be healthier than their predecessors, aging takes a toll on physical integrity, with mobility and vision issues causing severe inconvenience.

Some of the fastest-growing categories reside in their home improvement. One space where mobility can be a challenge is in the bathroom. Considerations such as lowered toilets, accessible bathtubs, and showers with no curbs add significant benefits and convenience in the bathroom, increasing safety in their residence.

Self-diagnostic care, with remote caregiver support is another category to grow. The automatic pill dispensing devices is a great space where the product can offer peace of mind for regular medication for seniors who live alone. A wearable self-diagnostic device on a patient will connect to caregivers, and it will monitor the clients' vital status at all times. AIP is a great space where the hardware and software can team up together to provide quality medical service. The product and service can reach seniors and be able to serve physical and emotional stability.

5. Software & Hardware

Steve Jobs, in his keynote in 2007, quotes Alan Kay that "People who are serious about software should make their own hardware." [67] As the software and digital contents on-screen prevails in our industry, hardware seems to support and negotiate with the practical side. As Steve Jobs asserted, suitable software should synchronize with a hardware design to do its best performance.[68] And proper hardware can double its value when equipped with great software. As Apple products are designed, the software and hardware seamlessly interrelate with each other, we will see more and more interdisciplinary works between software and hardware, which will yield significant value in the market.

---

[67] Alan Kay, a pioneer on object-oriented programming and windowing graphical user interface design

[68] Steve Jobs by Walter Issacson

6. POC (Proof of Concept)

Manufacturing in the near future will break the ground again and will let startups experience unprecedented product development. Digital clones will virtually manage production remotely, and they should be able to monitor job status on real-time dashboards. LVB (low volume build; small volume production, especially for startups) for POC (proof of concept) will be available for startups to verify their prototypes before they invest capital for mass production.

Low volume products will be possible by employing high-quality 3D printers, such as MJF (multi-jet fusion) type 3D printer, which can offer the production-grade parts in a short time. Besides that, we already see the multiple-axis CNC machine that mills the prototype in all directions, and the precision cutters precisely do a die-cut of the various material surfaces for the package. Designers will look for the advanced manufacturing technique of what they need rather than figuring out how to fit into the existing technology.

Intellectual Property

Design, to most people, is a subject matter. Some people value creative ideas, while others do not. Some consumers pay extra money to purchase value-added products and services, while others look for the cheapest option. Every consumer has a different value proposition when they shop for their needs. Thus, we see companies focusing on a strategic target with exclusively premium products that are unique and value-added. But how can we protect intellectual property?

Ownership

The product's intellectual property belongs to the company that owns it. In a highly competitive market, it is critical to protect the intellectual property that is developed by group activities, such as consumer research and design development. Designers everywhere share resources to inspire their work. Thus, they often conclude with great ideas, but very similar to what competitors already developed. The rule is the first to claim an idea takes ownership.

Patent

An intellectual property patent lawyer helps to protect and claim design ownership. For ownership, the design language must formulate in essence so that it can be documented. The US patent office requires a technical line drawing to identify the individual design language to differentiate one idea from another. This documentation needs to be endorsed by the designer, or inventor, to make its ownership active. [69]

Reward

"Never leave well enough alone." [70] It is hard to judge the perfect design. However, there is always a better design as much as the team puts design force on their product. As I talked about in 06_PROBLEM Creative Force, the creative energy can push the limit to go beyond competitors.

One of the challenges of design perfection is pursuing a simple design while integrating with the details. A simple design is not eliminating elements but keeping them in order, so users can approach those seamlessly when they need it. [71] The actual

---

[69] Design Patent Application Guide | USPTO
[70] Never leave well enough alone, 1951 by Raymond Loewy
[71] Jony Ive: The Genius Behind Apple's Greatest Products

design perfection, by far, is maintaining the balance between simplicity and product integrity for the consumers' best experiences. This process takes an effort and, often, dedication. Once the team reaches it, the reward can pay off.

Awards

There are multiple design awards for which the design team can apply. It is a great way to expose excellent design development to the public. The awarded product can be acknowledged and promoted for brand awareness and marketing. IDSA (International Design Society of America)[72] is an excellent institute for an annual product design award along with CES (Consumer Electronics Show) innovation design award. In Europe, iF and RedDot are two significant groups. They are both prestigious and well-reputed for judges and their promotion in the industry.

---

[72] A membership-based not-for-profit organization that promotes the practice and education of industrial design

| REMEMBER & USE |

Every team has development processes, but not all of them are capable of adopting change. Teams should be agile to disrupt the traditional process when it is necessary to meet consumers' needs in the rapidly changing market.
Innovation and concurrent engineering are great tools teams can consider. Using brainstorming, rapid prototyping, and checkpoints to meet deadlines will be helpful to move forward.

Markets are already pervasive with products, and the team should consider how to survive despite high competition. Research and competitive analysis are useful to forecast the market trends and will help teams to position the target market to succeed.

Teams should look at the new market and adopt changes by overlapping roles and responsibility to achieve business goals faster. Success belongs to who is initiating the action and protecting it. The design team should consider the intellectual property and should promote business by the excellence of the product and service.

OPEN-ENDED

Through my unique experiences as a designer, I like to make it clear that my journey did not need a destination, just like life. Every once in a while, we arrive at a checkpoint and unpack it to see what is inside. At each step, we share insights and reinforce them. The journey is exciting because it always opens up a new experience. And the experiences miraculously connect to tell a compelling story. When the journey is open-ended, growing is the only way.

MY JOURNEY

Why Design?

I became aware of the fascinating term, "design" when I was in middle school. I found the word quite peculiar, but my mind voluntarily associated it with slick electronics that work like magic. Sony CF-1980 cassette FM Radio was my favorite toy that showed me a circuit board, a cassette module, and sophisticated construction. While I was dissecting other electronics, a TV show featuring "Industrial Design" caught my attention, and the documentary immediately hooked me on how prosperous the industry would be in the future. As the show defined, the job creating purposeful and beautiful objects that have never existed before was so convincing that I made up my mind to pursue it as a life-time career.

Just like me, there are numerous designers around the world with this broad role that includes design development. Some projects took only a few weeks, which resulted in a crude solution, while other projects lasted a full year to develop a comprehensive product development. The problem is there are so many projects that they don't know how to manage the resources to get the best result.

One statistic says that there are over 30,000 new products introduced every year, and 95 percent of them fail.[73] Even the survivors are not guaranteed to offer a successful outcome. Indeed, the fascinating word brings people to Design, but many of them do not know how to plan the job to create a successful product. Industries are working in diverse design categories, such as services, electronics, consumables, medical devices, retail, and countless more. Our consumers are spectating how massive design outputs are in modern society and desperately looking for products that genuinely meet their needs.

People stereotypically think that design is an activity of product development that includes engineering (hardware and software) and styling. Some people think that design is engineering, while others perceive it as aesthetics on the product. As we are already living in the information era, it is exciting to see machine learning and self-driving. The industry is designing products that have never existed before. But what makes those designs unique and special? What makes consumers excited about new products? These questions still make design unclear, yet inevitable for me to answer.

---

[73] MarketSmart Newsletters, Lonny Kocina, May 3, 2017

From twenty years of field practice, I conclude all design development is a goal-directed play. Designers today should be more driven in answer to, 'How does design relate to people? [74] Having worked as a designer in excellent design teams, I have come up with how design is shaping the future of business and what ingredients are successfully guiding the design development. As a part of my career, I here share creative design principles and invaluable insights that can drive product design development. There is neither a correct nor wrong way to develop a product, but I hope Design Recipe will lead the right way of designing a successful product for you.

My Journey

My journey has been lucky to encounter great design communities and professionals that have shown me diverse cultures. It has been fascinating to observe many aspects of consumer perception, as I have gone through various projects.

As a native Korean, I was fortunate to start my professional career at Samsung and learned invaluable lessons about manufacturing methods and implementations. The philosophy of the production

---

[74] Victor Papanek, The Green Imperative

and its implementation have been significant assets. My graduate education at Pratt Institute, located in Brooklyn, was a pivotal moment in my life. The time was granted to me to form a broader vision of the pure aesthetics that the consumers value and appreciate for their lifestyle. Pratt's design program features one of pioneering design education, proudly focusing on the aesthetic design forces, some of which are addressed in 06_PROBLEM Creative Force in this book.

Joining design agencies opened a grand door to consumers and corporate brands. It was a game-changing experience and a privilege to focus on consumers and users. My colleagues reside in the heart of the design activities, and they have been teaching me with insights and motivations.

The transition from the Pacific Northwest to the East Coast and back to the center of Silicon Valley was a phenomenal experience to confront the distinct cultural differences. People, languages, foods, politics, value propositions, and much more are fascinating and overwhelming experiences in my journey. And I have come up with the opportunity to share these lessons in return.